The Christ-centered Family

Raymond T. Brock

Radiant BOOKS

Gospel Publishing House/Springfield, Mo. 65802

02-0903

THE CHRIST-CENTERED FAMILY
© 1977 by the Gospel Publishing House
Springfield, Missouri 65802

Library of Congress Catalog Card Number 76-46036
International Standard Book Number 0-88243-903-0
Printed in the United States of America

A teacher's guide for group study with this book is available from the Gospel Publishing House (order number 32-0173).

Contents

One Plus One Equals One

Marriage Is Elective

YES, MARRIAGE IS ELECTIVE. It is not a required course in life. Not everyone marries; not everyone needs or wants to. For the majority of us, however, marriage is a God-given choice that we accept as a blessing from our Father in heaven who loves us and has given us the capacity to share love with Him and with a person of the complementary sex who He brings into our lives (Genesis 1:26, 27; 2:18, 21-25).

By the early 1970's there were almost 209 million people in the United States. Of this population half were between the ages of 15 and 54, the years of most active sexual activity. The rate of marriage per 1000 population was 11, indicating that almost 3 million married during 1 year alone.

Among American men ages 15 to 54 the average population breaks down as follows: about 23% single 67% married only once, 10% married more than once. (It is obvious that a large number of the single males are in their teens and too young to establish a meaningful marriage relationship.)

For women, the statistics vary a little. The single population between ages 15 and 54 accounted for about 18%, allowing for the female part of the population to marry younger than the male. Those married only once amounted to about 86% and those married twice or more represented about 15% of the population. Acknowledging that women frequently outlive their husbands the data also indicates that about 12% of those ever married were widowed and 15% were divorced.

Not only is marriage increasing; the number of divorces is also increasing. The divorce rate in 1972 represented 4 per 1000 population. The sobering fact growing out of these figures is that the average length of marriage in the U.S. is only 7 years. What a far cry from the Biblical injunction: "For this cause shall a man leave father and mother, and shall cleave to his wife: and they twain shall be one flesh. Wherefore they are no more twain but one flesh. What therefore God hath joined together, let not man put asunder" (Matthew 19:5, 6).

Preparing for Marriage

For a man to face marriage with emotional and spiritual maturity he needs to learn to be a trusting person who is motivated to develop himself to the best of his capacity. He must take the initiative in preparing for the responsibilities that go with the privileges of marriage and develop the work productiveness that makes it possible for him to provide for a wife and family. The wife, on the other hand, must prepare herself as adequately in the gifts and talents that lead to creative homemaking and parenting.

Unless each member of the marriage partnership sees himself in a mature role as male or female problems are inevitable. It is in knowing who you are, where you are going, and what the Lord is enabling you to become that marriage takes on its highest meaning. It is basically the absence of mistrust, doubt, shame, guilt, feelings of inferiority, and other attitudes and emotions that fragment relationships (Romans 8:14-17).

It is more important to *become* the right person for marriage than it is to *find* the right partner in marriage. This includes an acceptance of yourself as an adequately functioning person. To be an adequate marriage partner you must find a quiet pleasure in being yourself and not be wishing you were someone else or like someone else. Then you must reach out and extend yourself to others in the selflessness that makes you sensitive to their needs as well as your own. Otherwise you live closer to the animal level than the human level of existence.

Genesis 1 specifically indicates that human creation was different in time and character from that of the animal world. God spoke animals into being (Genesis 1:24, 25). He formed man out of the dust of the earth and then breathed into the clay model of the human tabernacle the breath of life (Genesis 1:26, 27; 2:7). It is this image of the divine in us that makes us the ultimate perfection of God's creative genius.

Do you enjoy being with people? Do you relate warmly and genuinely to them? This is essential to becoming the right person for marriage. If you can relate to others adequately then you are well on the way to the openness to life's experiences that allows you to feel all of your sensory and emotional sensations and respond to them with excitement. God has given us the capacity to relate to Him sincerely, to others warmly, and to our spouse (husband or wife) tenderly. It is in the intimate sharings of marriage that the highest human experiences are enjoyed with a loved partner of the complementary sex as a sacrament of praise to God who has so endowed us with the capacity for this fulfillment.

Be Objective About Yourself

To keep marriage alive it is necessary to be objective about yourself. It is far too easy to see things as you feel they are, not as they actually are. To be objective about yourself requires both insight and humor. Insight is the ability to see yourself as you really are and to understand your motivations. This brings into harmony what *you are,* what *you think you are,* and what *others think you are.* These are not necessarily the same view of self unless you are being transparent with others and honest with yourself.

Humor is essential to the vitality of marriage. It involves the ability to see light when it is dark, to laugh when you are sad, and to find joy in living —sometimes in spite of adverse circumstances. Without humor, a marriage dies. To be able to see the ridiculous in some of the things you do and say and what others do and say takes the tension out of many stressful situations. And it is good for your health. It is physically impossible to burn an ulcer while you are laughing. Nature won't let you activate the nerve that sends the excess gastric juices into your stomach to burn the ulcer while you are laughing. So keep the humor in your marriage and you will enjoy better physical health.

One other point of view will help you become the right person for marriage. Live in the real present, not in the memories of the past or fantasies of the future. Reality orientation involves being in close touch with the real world in which you live. This brings you above the childlike ties to family and nature and allows you to transcend the carnal self to identify with the divine capacity to see yourself as both subject and agent of your own powers, to be aware of what is going on inside of you and outside of you at the same time. Monitoring internal emotions in light of external realities is essential for good marital relationships. It keeps you alive and gives you the ability to live as unto the Lord intently and honestly.

Ensuring Success

I believe that any two normal Christian adults of complementary sexes can have a successful marriage.

First, each of the couple must be *physically normal* and desire to share in heterosexual marriage. This desire is God-given. When God saw Adam alone in the garden of Eden with all the animals of the world, He realized this human creature had no one with whom to share intellectual stimulation, spiritual companionship, and physical intimacy. So, in His divine love, God created a helper adequate to meet Adam's needs (Genesis 2:18, 21-23).

With physical normalcy as a basis the next consideration in marriage is the sharing of *Christian values.* It is in the spiritual union of a couple that the basis for happiness really lies. Those marriages that are complicated with a difference in religious affiliation, values, and attitudes are subject to many more frustrations than those in which the couple agree on Christ as Lord, the church in which they will worship, and the kind of values they will share in family worship. Religious differences in marriage lead to much unhappiness for the couple and create many questions in the minds of children which lead to problems in establishing their own values in later life.

The third consideration is that of being *mature adults*. After all marriage is for adults. It is when the immature behaviors of childhood creep into what should be mature problem solving that much anxiety emerges.

A 3-year-old throws a tantrum and falls on the floor. We say, "Isn't she cute. Just like her mother's side of the family." No, it's not cute and it isn't from anyone's side of the family. Immature behavior is prevalent in us all until we learn the disciplines of maturing into adulthood. But when the married person of 23 or 33 or 43 or older reverts to the tantrums of the 3-year-old, problems are inevitable. Marriage is for adults and requires adult handling of problems. Otherwise, fragmentation begins with the accompanying unhappiness.

Why Marry?

The question is often asked, why marry? Why not just live together? The Bible is explicit in reasons for marriage and replete with illustrations of what happens when individuals take sexual privileges without the sanctity of Christian marriage.

Psychologically, invasion of the private physical dignity of another person without the commitment of marriage violates the essence of being. It reduces the individual to being nothing more than a thing, an object for the gratification of biological impulses. This form of existence is no higher than the animal world and certainly beneath the dignity of God's highest creation. Shattered relics of promiscuous sex fill our mental institutions and account for a significant portion of our growing suicide rate.

10

Kenneth Gangel in *The Family First* (Minneapolis: HIS International Service, 1972) offers four reasons for Christian marriage: fellowship, sexual fulfillment, procreation, and an example to the world. I should like to offer a fifth, division of labor, as a result of my overseas travels.

Fellowship. God saw that it was not good for man to be alone. He needed someone with whom he could communicate, fellowship, and share communion (Genesis 2:18).

Open communication is essential in marriage. It should begin early in dating. Marriage counselors tell us that 85 percent of the problems leading to divorce begin with faulty communication. Not sex. Not money. Not in-laws. Inability to communicate shatters relationships. That is why it is so important for prospective brides and grooms to check their communication patterns and be sure that intellectually, spiritually, and socially they are on the same wave length and can be honest in sharing their hopes and fears, joys and sorrows.

The Physical Side

Sexual fulfillment. God created woman to be the mirror image of man. One is incomplete without the other, physically and psychologically, but together they become one unit (Genesis 2:24, 25; Matthew 19:5, 6). That is why the Epistles teach that marriage is honorable and sexual activity between a Christian husband and wife is an act of worship that the Lord has blessed (Hebrews 13:4). So much is sexual fulfillment the privilege of the Christian married couple that they are cautioned against withholding sexual fulfillment from their lover for any reason, except for a spiritual fast, and that fast should be of very short duration (1 Corinthians 7:1-5).

Dwight Small in *Christian: Celebrate Your Sexuality* (Old Tappan, NJ: Fleming H. Revell Co., 1974) observes that "our culture has succeeded in squeezing sex into a mold that is too small for it, making it less than the Creator intended it to be." On the other hand, he says, "Sexuality is an expression of the whole person; it belongs to the symphony of human existence. It cannot be compartmentalized, but is the music of the body complete with rhythms and melodies and harmonies. Throughout the relationship of marriage there plays, as it were, the obbligato of sexual love." He is saying that God expects the sexual relationship to mean more than just physical responses.

Procreation. Children are to be viewed as a blessing from the Lord. Nowhere in the Bible does God restrict sexual fulfillment to procreation. On the other hand, the Word does point out that children are a blessing and should be received as God's gift to parents (Genesis 1:26-28; Psalms 127, 128). The one caution the Bible has is that the number of children should be planned within the ability of the parents to provide for the intellectual, spiritual, and physical welfare of their family (1 Timothy 5:8).

Family planning is a spiritual concern when sexual fulfillment in Christian marriage is seen as a God-given privilege to be enjoyed apart from the specific occasion when children are desired. Hannah sought the Lord and Samuel was born. Abraham received Isaac as a divine sign. Elisabeth conceived miraculously.

Example to the world. Of all the institutions God has established, He uses marriage to illustrate the mystery of eternity. He likens the love Christ has for the Church to the love a Christian husband and wife should share for each other. As an example to the world, the Christian husband is to demonstrate sacrificial love for his wife and to minister as priest and spiritual leader of his household (Ephesians 5:20-33). Notice the sequence of expanding loving relationships.

(1) A man is admonished to love his wife as he loves himself, to nourish and cherish and take as good care of her as he does of himself. (2) Then he is to love his wife as Christ loved the Church—to the point of death—giving his last ounce of strength for her. It is to the wife that is so loved that the Apostle says: "Wives, submit yourselves unto your own husbands, as unto the Lord" (Ephesians 5:22). Submissive not because the man is male or superior, but as unto the Lord who is over all (1 Peter 3:1).

The wife who is loved as Christ wants her to be loved enjoys the cooperative freedoms that are her privilege because she is married to a man who is loving her in the way Christ wants her to be loved. After all, in God there is neither male nor female—that is, all are equal in His sight (Galatians 3:28).

Division of labor. This last point is added after sharing the concepts of this chapter with national Christians in Africa, Latin America, and Asia. Culture places certain demands on men and women. These are not divine imperatives, but are cultural expectations. God's Word is universal. It is not the

13

private book of any culture, race, language, or people.

When culture has assigned specific tasks to members of the household, these should be examined carefully and carried out as unto the Lord. The New Testament is full of teachings of how to be Christlike within cultural expectations.

Whereas in Nigeria it is a cultural expectation for women to cook, sew, farm, and trade in the markets, the same is not necessarily true in the United States or Canada. Even subcultures in North America have their own expectations. The professional woman, for instance, has certain expectations to live up to on the job and another set to implement at home. Each of us has to work out his own job assignment for the welfare of the family, making sure the spiritual life of the family does not suffer as we ply our individual interests and pursuits.

In the U.S., for instance, only one job is sex-specific. Women will do the childbearing. But, men are much involved in the rearing of children as well as working in the home and its environs as the family works together to be a unit. It is in the togetherness of working and playing together that love grows and security in the Christian home is established.

CHAPTER TWO

Making Marriage Christian

First Things First

AS WAS HIS CUSTOM, JESUS was frequently in dialogue with religious leaders and the common people. On one occasion, a young scribe came up to the group gathered around Jesus. After hearing how the Lord met His distractors, the scribe asked, "Which is the first commandment of all?" (Mark 12:28).

In so many words the young man was saying, "Master, I can't handle 10 commandments all at once, where do I begin?" Jesus was very specific in His response: "The first of all the commandments is, Hear, O Israel: the Lord our God is one Lord: and thou shalt love the Lord thy God with all thy heart, and with all thy soul, and with all thy mind, and with all thy strength: this is the first commandment" (Mark 12:29, 30). Jesus was quoting from Deuteronomy 6:4, 5.

Loving God adequately is essential if we are going to love each other effectively. Before we can look at the love between the Christian husband and wife, it is essential to look at the love life of the Christian and his God.

Heart

What does it mean to love God with the "heart"? This refers to the part of the intelligence that has to do with knowledge, understanding, and knowing not only what the Word says but also what it means in everyday life.

Paul picks up this concept in 2 Timothy 2:15 when he tells us to study God's Word to such a degree that we can apply it accurately in everyday life. Why? Because God's Word was given under the inspiration of the Holy Spirit to give us the information needed to handle life's problems (3:16, 17).

When we love God with the heart, we use the Bible as a basis for planning our daily lives. His Word is *doctrine*, the basis of teaching truth (John 16:13). Letting God's Word be the core of shared values brings harmony into marriage. It gives us the guidelines we need to bring our lives under the control of His Spirit and teaches us how to walk in His ways.

Scripture has also been given to us for *reproof*. This refers specifically to preventive information given to keep us from falling into error. It also censures our lives when we have made a mistake. When a couple desires God's will with all their hearts, they will be open to the leadership of the Holy Spirit to bring the Word to their remembrance and help them avoid mistakes.

Correction, a third application of the Word to the heart that loves God, points out the errors of our ways. Whether it be an intentional or unintentional wrong, the applying of the Word to the heart of the Christian husband or wife brings a quick apology and the restoring of relationships (Ephesians 4:25-

27). Quick reconciliation for inconsiderations keeps little misdemeanors from becoming big problems.

Finally, knowing the Word of God opens our hearts to the *instruction* of the Lord. It makes us open to the new things He wants to teach us as our love grows for Him and for one another.

To love God with all the heart, then, means to study God's Word and let its pages come alive so the Holy Spirit can lead us into all truth. A husband and wife who share a love of God based on His Word and a love for each other that allows His love to mature, are well on their way to knowing the ultimate joy in marriage.

Soul

Loving God with the soul involves the will, affection, desire, and the whole realm of our emotions. David struck a beautiful note when he said, "Unto thee, O Lord, do I lift up my soul," and, "I delight to do thy will, O my God" (Psalms 25:1; 40:8).

To desire to know the will of God is the highest ambition; to do the will of God is the greatest accomplishment. Count Von Zinzendorf, founder of the great Moravian Missionary Society of the 18th century, had as his motto for life: "I have one passion—it is Christ and He alone." No loftier goal could be set in Christian marriage than to so love God with all of the heart. This stimulates the motivation of His love to bring happiness into the life of our companion.

It is in loving God with our whole heart that we are able to bring our own desires in Christian marriage under the control of the Holy Spirit and seek to fulfill His divine will as we meet the needs of the one He has given us.

Mind

It is interesting to note that "mind" is not listed in the Deuteronomy passage from which Jesus was quoting. The ancient Hebrew did not distinguish between the body, soul, and spirit. He saw them as a unit, not separate entities. The influence of Greek philosophy, however, had crept into Jewish tradition by the time of Jesus, and the distinction between heart and mind was common. To accommodate himself to the people, Jesus took the intent of the *Shema* (the Deuteronomy passage) as it had been given by God and interpreted it in the language of the people to whom He was speaking.

When Jesus used the word *mind* He was speaking of the part of the intelligence that involves wisdom. Divine wisdom comes from above (Proverbs 2:6). It is the result of first, revelation and, second, experience. Hard as it is to accept, nothing comes into the life of the believer without the presence of the Father. If we can learn to accept the events of life as gifts from God to demonstrate new revelations of His love for us, we will find that the fear (reverence, respect) of the Lord is the beginning of wisdom (Psalm 111:10).

Not only does the Lord want us to learn wisdom from the things that happen to us, He wants us to profit from the experiences of others—vicarious learning. Learning the lessons of history is not always easy, but it is essential if we are going to profit from the past.

This is especially true in marriage. When we learn to love the Lord with all our heart, we will be able to take His Word and apply it to our daily lives. Profiting from the mistakes and successes of others, as the Holy Spirit gives us the written record, affords us the opportunity to apply the experiences of the past to the challenges of the present. This is the kind of loving and living that makes the Christian marriage the happiest in the community.

Strength

Now the Lord moves to our energy supply. To love the Lord with our energy involves giving all that we are to Him in behavioral demonstration of the love that is developing in our heart: to put His will first in our time and work. When we demonstrate our love for Him by practical involvement in His work, we find new ways to love Him in service. So Paul challenges us to do all things to the glory of God (1 Corinthians 10:38).

Loving God with the heart, soul, and mind is all internal. It is only as we have transferred these cognitive and affective attitudes into action that others can see the depth of our love for God. And when we love God in the way He wants us to love Him, we turn our attention to the partner He has given us and demonstrate this love as a spontaneous outflow of the heart that loves God adequately and then turns to love a lover effectively.

When Jesus quoted from the *Shema* in response to the inquiry of the scribe, He quickly summarized the rest of the Law: "And the second is like, namely this, Thou shalt love thy neighbor as thyself" (Mark 12:31). In this declaration Jesus summarized the essence of the Decalogue. But the question arises, "Who is my neighbor?" Since Jesus was dealing with relationships close to home, we should start the consideration of neighbor love with the neighbor that is closest to us.

19

Spouse

Who is your closest neighbor? Your husband or wife, your spouse. In Western countries individuals elect from among their neighbors one they will elevate to the position of marriage partner. In other cultures, such arrangements may be made by families through traditional negotiations. It really doesn't matter whether the husband and wife have come together according to cultural customs or romantic dating; any two normal Christian adults of complementary sexes can have a successful marriage.

Although this concept seems strange to the Western mind where so much emphasis is on romantic love, the fact remains that two individuals who love God the way He should be loved—with the heart, soul, mind, and strength—are going to join their energies in serving Him adequately and find that their love is growing as they put Christ in the center of their relationship.

The wife that is loved in the way Christ wants her to be loved finds joy in being submissive in the interactions of marriage because both husband and wife are responding as unto the Lord. Submission here is not to a man because he is male or superior, but to being a loving wife who has the privilege of being loved by a Christian husband in the way Christ wants her to be loved.

Not only will she be submissive to the opportunities of making her husband and children happy, but she will demonstrate before them a reverential love that will encourage the children to respect their father. A wife who is so loved has not surrendered her freedom. Rather, she is the most liberated woman in the world. She can develop her own abilities as God has endowed her and can cooperate without inhibition with her husband in Christian marriage.

Children

To the couple who loves God in the way He should be loved and are loving each other as a spontaneous outflow of their affection for each other, their next closest neighbor is their own children. They see that their responsibility before God is to set an example of obedience to God in the divine order of relationships and to bring up their children "in the nurture and admonition of the Lord" (Ephesians 6:4).

How? By making God's Word the guideline for living. Parents must study God's Word systematically and apply it in daily life, for it is the best book written on child rearing (2 Timothy 2:15; 3:16, 17). Parents who study God's Word as their guidebook for leading young lives are equipped to lead them, as did Mary and Joseph, to mature mentally, physically, spiritually, and socially (Luke 2:52).

Extended Family

Not only does the Lord want us to love our immediate families, He wants us to maintain positive relations with members of the extended family on both sides. The in-law relationships must be constantly revised. The Christian husband is not only a son but becomes a son-in-law. This is a new relationship for both the old and the new generations and must be cultivated as part of Christian marriage.

Ruth loved her mother-in-law so much she forsook her pagan Moab to move to the hills of Judea after the death of her husband. Peter was concerned enough about his mother-in-law to ask Jesus to pray for her healing. The older woman arose from her bed and prepared dinner for Jesus and His disciples. Timothy's continued relationship with his mother and grandmother was eulogized by the apostle Paul.

It is true that Jesus reiterated the command of God that the young couple should forsake father and mother and cleave only to each other, but He did not release them from the responsibility of loving and taking care of the older generation. Love without meddling—this is the privilege of loving relationships through the extended family.

Church

As the new home is established, God wants the young couple to maintain their contact with the church and to remain active in Christian service. It is a disastrous mistake for young lovers to become so absorbed in their new relationship and stabilizing their jobs and working on their own personal adjustments that they forsake the house of the Lord. Rather, God would have the young couple take their new privilege in Christ and bring their energies to bear on the work of the church.

No church will be stronger than the marriages upon which it is founded. The family that puts Christ first in all their activities will find that it is in their togetherness in spiritual worship and witnessing that their love can grow and they can become in Christ what they are capable of becoming. Rather than limiting their freedom and tying them down, their involvement in church gives them a platform from which to be God's hand extended into a community that needs Christ. Involvement in Christian service cements relationships and makes marriage more actively Christian.

Community

With their different community involvements the couple must be discriminating about where they will put their time and energies. The Lord wants us to be concerned with the lost and to measure our community and civic involvements in relationship to the time and money we have. When we order our priorities so that our love for Him is first, our love for each other is second, and our children are given the kind of loving direction they need, Christian service through the church and community becomes a pleasure.

However, outreach should never drain energies from the primary relationships. We are commanded to be witnesses to the whole world, but we must not forsake our Jerusalem—our own families—in our eagerness to reach out to the exotic and different.

Loving God in the way He should be loved is the secret of having Christ in the home. The home that is founded on a sincere love for God gives the liberty to love each other selflessly as God intended. This kind of relationship encompasses the children, the members of the extended family, and through the church, the community. Then the desire of Jesus is fulfilled: "This is my commandment, That ye love one another, as I have loved you" (John 15:12). This is love to the point of total sacrifice that divine love may flow. This is the kind of love that makes marriage Christian.

CHAPTER THREE

Your Closest Neighbor

Complementary—Not Opposite

A fellow and a girl who wed
Begin to live as one 'tis said
But many couples can't agree
Which one of them they wish to be.

YOUR CLOSEST NEIGHBOR IS YOUR SPOUSE (husband or wife), the one you elected as partner for life. God has created us as *complementary* sexes, not opposite sexes, to establish the relationship of marriage.

Too often people refer to their mate as the opposite sex. This implies the kind of differences that lead to sparring or fighting and is as far from God's divine intent as a concept can be. He made us complementary sexes, mirror images of each other physically and emotionally, so that we can make each other complete.

God put Adam to sleep and took a major portion of his side from which to create Eve. The word *rib* means "flank." It indicates that God took not only bone but muscle, tendon, flesh, and skin from which to form his crowning creation. When Adam looked on the beautiful creature his response was approval (Genesis 2:23, 25).

The philosopher and theologian Augustine observed early in church history: "If God meant woman to rule over man, He would have taken her out of Adam's head. Had He designed her to be his slave, He would have taken her out of his feet. But God took woman out of man's side, for He made her to be a helpmate and an equal of him." Years later Myer Pearlman observed that woman was taken from under the arm of man to be protected by him and from near his heart to be loved by him.

It is in this complementary relationship of equality that partners in Christian marriage have their highest anticipations and broadest liberties (Galatians 3:28).

Consider a lock and key. They are a functioning unit. Each can exist independently, but together they accomplish a purpose. Neither is superior. Each is essential. Two locks do not fit; two keys do not function. Even a lock and a key that are not properly matched do not work.

When we allow the Spirit of the Lord to mold our personalities to conform to His image, He brings the blend of our lives to conform to His will. When we each are being molded by the Holy Spirit, our lives will blend as the key in the lock to unlock for us the riches of the kingdom of heaven.

Differences Between the Sexes

Differences between the sexes lend excitement to marriage. It is well known that men are usually bigger and heavier than their spouses, capable of heavier work and greater stamina. On the other hand, it is the tenderness of women that compensates for the brusqueness of men and balances the psychological atmosphere of the home. Whereas men pride themselves on their logical thought processes, it is the intuitive nature of women to handle the ambiguities of marriage and family.

Men are known for their aggressiveness in sports, business, and warfare, whereas women are expected to be more adaptable to new situations. One thing they share in common, however, is fragile egos. Each can be easily offended in ways the other finds it difficult to understand. Problems arise when a woman uses her typically indirect approach to a husband that is used to the frontal attack in the masculine world. Hints go unheeded and the result is assumed neglect. The attitudes of Romans 12:10 are vital in marital relations at this point.

Another area of concern is in the reluctance with which men express their emotions and admit to their feelings. They find it difficult to handle a wife who legitimately gives free expression to such emotions as fear, pity, sadness, and affection, especially to others of the same sex.

One of the new trends in Western child rearing is fortunate. More and more little boys are being allowed to express their emotions, especially to cry when they are hurt. The old reprimand, "Big boys don't cry," has led to men who find it impossible to admit and express their emotions. Unfortunately, little boys who don't learn to cry honestly grow up to become men who find it difficult to express their emotions in the affectionate ways that are appropriate in Christian marriage. The Scriptures support masculine expressions of honest emotion (Genesis 37:34; 1 Samuel 18:3; Luke 19:41; John 11:35).

Levels of Love

How much should a man love his wife? At least as much as he loves himself. Paul points out in Ephesians 5:28, 29 that a man loves himself enough to nourish and take good care of himself. Why? Self-preservation. So, it is required of the Christian husband that he love his wife at least as much as he loves himself; to take good physical care of his wife and provide for her needs.

But, for the Christian wife, nurturing is not enough. Paul goes a step further and says that a Christian husband should love his wife as much as Christ loved the Church. How much did Jesus love the Church? To the point of death! (Ephesians 5:25). It is in loving his wife to his last ounce of strength that a Christian husband demonstrates the sincerity of his love and the integrity of his own relationship with Christ.

How, then, does the Christian wife who is so loved respond to her husband? Ephesians 5:22-24, 33 gives insight into the matter.

This is not submission to a man because he is male or because he is bigger or superior. It is submission to the relationship of being joint-heirs to the promises of the kingdom of God and being submissive unto God who has assigned us our roles in divine relationships.

Submission is unto God. The loving husband is the catalyst that brings out this loving demonstration that inspires respect (reverence) in a wife who is being loved as sincerely and deliberately as Christ has ordained.

It has frequently been noted that Scripture does not command a wife to love her husband. That command was not necessary because the wife who is loved as Christ wants her to be loved cannot resist the husband who is loving her with divine love. The response of love to Christ brings love as a spontane-

27

ous outflow of the personality into the marital relationship. But, lest there be a question of how long this kind of love should last, Paul said the older women of the church should teach the younger women to love their husbands and children (Titus 2:4).

If there is a God-given maternal instinct that brings love spontaneously out of the heart of the new mother, so the same capacity is there for loving a husband who is setting the example of loving, tender concern.

One other option is available, but it is inferior: "Love your enemies" (Matthew 5:44). Then the Lord proceeds to tell us how to initiate reconciliation when fragmentation has ruptured relationships.

So, for the Christian there is only one way—the way of love for a lifetime. If, through sin and waywardness, relationships are ruptured so that former lovers become enemies, there is a spiritual way to restore the relationship.

The husband who respects himself enough to respect his wife should seek the Lord for the graces and virtues to love her in the way Christ wants her to be loved. Then he can know the highest form of human love, the love that symbolizes the mystical relationship between Christ and His Church. This is the love that lasts for a lifetime and remains in the glow of memories after death has intervened.

Compatible Relationships

Thousands of years separate the 20th-century marriage from Biblical illustrations. However, there is precedent for exploring the dimensions of love in the marital relationships of saints in ages past. As with all human beings, their love was imperfect, but it gives us guidelines for confronting contemporary problems by profiting from ancient experiences.

Abraham and Sarah were not perfect lovers. Although they traversed hundreds of miles together, when the angel predicted the birth of Isaac, Sarah found it difficult to maintain the faith of her husband (Genesis 18:9-15). Yet, she is extolled by Peter as an example of submission to the privileges and responsibilities of being a wife (1 Peter 3:6). Her basic attitudes seem to have been right even if she occasionally doubted some of the dimensions of her husband's faith.

Elisabeth and Zechariah represent as compatible a human relationship as the Bible describes. Their communication seems to be open and accepting. It was only when Zechariah had difficulty accepting the total message of the angel concerning the birth of John the Baptist that the frustrating temporary muteness entered their marriage, but it seems to have put no strain on the relationship (Luke 1:5-25, 57-66).

Hannah and Elkanah also seemed to maintain a positive relationship, although she desired a child so much it caused a problem. The supportiveness of their relationship tolerated the strain of the childless years, the separations of Hannah remaining home when Elkanah went to the temple when Samuel was a child, and then the annual treks to take the young priest new garments (1 Samuel 1; 2:19).

Strained Relationships

Although it did not break them up, Isaac and Rebekah had a strained relationship. They started out on what seemed to be a fairy-tale romance. She came by camel train to meet a husband about whom she knew nothing except stories she had heard. She gave up family, culture, and civilization for a fantasy that exceeded her fondest imaginations (Genesis 24). However, hers was a deceitful love (see lesson 7) and she was caught in the deceit of trying to get Jacob the birthright Isaac had promised to Esau (Genesis 27). Living in such duplicity taught the boys a kind of deception that accompanied them throughout their adult years.

The story of David and Michal is another with a storybook beginning. Poor shepherd boy marries into royalty (1 Samuel 18:20, 21). But hers was a romanticized love (see lesson 7). When the flame of romance flickered, what had been love turned to hate as she saw her king-husband in a spontaneous act of worship (2 Samuel 6:16).

The illicit love affair between Samson and Delilah professed a love that was conditional. Their entire relationship was marked by challenge and questions (Judges 16:4-19). The constant placing of tests to prove love made it impossible for love to mature between them. They were in constant battle for superiority, a battle which ended in Samson's death.

Another strained relationship was that of David and Bathsheba, which illustrates a self-seeking, neurotic love (2 Samuel 11:2-27). In taking another man's wife, David grossly sinned. Arranging for Uriah's death by proxy, however, was even worse. God's hand in judgment came on the house when the child was taken in death in infancy (2 Samuel 12:15-23).

Severed Relationships

God never intended for divorce to interrupt marriage. The result of such a rupture brings profound tragedy, leaving only anguish, bitterness, loneliness, and a sense of failure for all concerned. Jesus emphasized that it was only due to the hardness of the human heart that Moses allowed the granting of a bill of divorcement.

Malachi 2:14-16 indicates that God hates divorce. The statement on divorce adopted by the General Council in session in 1973 states: "This passage shows that divorce is treachery (deceitful unfaithfulness) against your companion."* And, worst of all, "Broken homes do not tend to produce the healthiest offspring . . . Divorce was not in God's original intention for man" (Matthew 19:6).

The Old Testament restricted divorce. "In giving Israel the Law, God accepted people where they were, put restrictions on their wrong practices, and tried to direct them."

"In their confrontation with Jesus on the question of divorce the Pharisees were obviously in error when they said that Moses *commanded* a man to give a certificate of divorce when putting his wife away (divorcing her). Jesus indicated that Moses only 'suffered' or permitted them to do so, and then, not for 'every cause' as was commonly practiced at that time" (Matthew 19:7, 8).

"This is borne out in Deuteronomy 21:1-4. The Hebrew Moses used here is a simple sequence that does not command divorce. He just recognizes that men were divorcing their wives." The only reason allowed was ". . . some moral or sexual uncleanness apart from adultery, since adultery would call for her death under the Law."

Jesus forbade divorce (Matthew 19:5 6; Mark 10:6-9) and so did Paul (1 Corinthians 7:10, 11). "Although Paul recognized that Christians were getting divorces he commanded that they keep the way open for reconciliation." Paul further forbids Christians to take the initiative in getting a divorce on the grounds that their partner is not a Christian (1 Corinthians 7:12-16).

On the other hand, Jesus permitted a Christian to initiate divorce proceedings when sexual infidelity was involved (Matthew 5:32; 19:9). Notice that this is by permission, not a command. By way of explanation it should be noted that "the Greek word for 'fornication' (*porneia*) may include especially repeated acts of adultery but usually means habitual sexual immorality of any kind both before and after marriage."

The Law permitted remarriage after divorce (Deuteronomy 24:1-4), but a priest was forbidden to take a divorced woman as his wife (Leviticus 21:7).

Jesus, in His basic teaching forbade remarriage of the divorced person (Mark 10:11, 12; Luke 16:18) but added an exceptive clause (Matthew 5:32) which shows that "a husband who divorces a sexually immoral woman does not cause her to commit adultery, since she is already guilty of adultery." Another exception is noted in Matthew 19:9. "It should be emphasized that the exception has in view sexual immorality, not merely a single act. Wherever possible, sexually immoral practices should be dealt with through repentance, confession, forgiveness, and reconciliation, thus saving the marriage."

God's plan is love and marriage for as long as both shall live. Not only is marriage for adults; marriage is for a lifetime. As Elizabeth Barrett Browning phrases it:

How do I love thee? Let me count the ways.
I love thee to the depth and breadth and height
My soul can reach, when feeling out of sight.
For the ends of Being and ideal Grace.
I love thee to the level of everyday's
Most quiet need by sun and candle-light.
I love thee freely, as men strive for Right;
I love thee purely, as they turn from Praise,
I love thee with the passion put to use
In my old griefs and with my childhood's faith.
I love thee with a love I seem to lose
With my lost saints,—I love thee with the breath,
Smiles, tears, of all my life!—and if God choose,
I shall but love thee better after death.

---

*This and other quoted material in this section is taken from The General Council of the Assemblies of God report on *Divorce and Remarriage*, August 21, 1973. It is available from the General Secretary's Office, 1445 Boonville Ave., Springfield, Mo. 65802.

CHAPTER FOUR
Like Parent, Like Child

A Sacred Trust

CHILDREN ARE A SACRED TRUST given by God to the
family, be they natural born or adopted (Psalm
127:3). Studies indicate it does not affect the happiness of the couple whether they bear children or not.
If both want children and keep their hearts open to
receive the new life as a gift from the Lord, they can
be happy whether or not they bear their own children. It is when one member of the marriage wants
children and the other does not that problems are apt
to arise in the relationship.

Many families who, for biological reasons, cannot
have children seek to adopt. Others turn their energies to' Christian service and become spiritual parents to the children and youth of the church. This is
an individual matter left to the discretion of the
couple. Those who seek to adopt, however, need to
examine their motives to make sure their desire is
not just to conform to the pattern of other couples or
because of peer pressure to have a child. Couples
must want children for the privilege of bringing
them up in the fear and admonition of the Lord;
otherwise, the adoption will be a fiasco.

Modeling Behavior

Effective discipline in the Christian home is the introduction of control into the life of a child. This is best accomplished by parents demonstrating before their children the kinds of self-discipline and self-control that are conducive to wholesome living (Matthew 5:16; Ephesians 6:4; Colossians 3:21).

The cliche: "What you are speaks so loudly I can't hear what you say," is uniquely true in the Christian home. Parents who want their children to be peaceable and in command of their own behavior must set the example of orderly living. Young lives are patterned after adult models.

The secret to discipline in the Christian home lies in establishing the divine order of relationships (Ephesians 5:21, 24; 6:1). As parents see their position as models for children in being submissive to God's authority in personal and family living, they set the example of disciplined living for their young.

Actually, parents can expect no more obedience from their children than they themselves demonstrate to the laws of the God whom they profess to serve. When there is a breakdown of cooperation in the Christian home, parents would do well to check their relationship with God to see if obedience is really the keynote of their own lives. It is in following the example of parents in being submissive to God's will that young lives learn to obey God. In honoring parents they learn obedience to the laws of God.

Fulfilling the commandment to honor and obey parents (Ephesians 6:1-3; Colossians 3:20) requires that children see the kind of discipline in the lives of their parents that merits honor and engenders obedience. Disobedience must have been rampant in Moses' day because of the promise attached to the commandment regarding parent-child relationships (Exodus 20:12).

The balance in relationships comes when parents set positive examples rather than engaging in activities that provoke children or drive them to rebellion (Ephesians 6:4; Colossians 3:21). The implication is that big folk don't do things to little folk just because they are bigger. Rather, parents set positive examples that lead young lives in the path they should follow. There is no substitute for teaching by example as far as discipline is concerned (Ephesians 5:15).

The sequence is developmental: children who honor their parents and obey them are motivated by parents who withhold provocation as they demonstrate the disciplines of the Holy Spirit in their own personal lives.

Making Disciples

The root for the word *discipline* is "discipling." To make disciples is to inspire followers. Parents who set the example of self-discipline have children who learn early the introduction of control that makes them capable of handling the problems of life.

Probably the most difficult part of being a loving parent is to be able to develop a system of reinforcements in the home that is a balance between rewarding acceptable behavior and withholding overt acts of love in order to help the child learn more appropriate ways of behaving.

The parent who loves the child but disapproves of disobedient behavior can assure the child that he is loved at all times and still teach that disobedience is not to be tolerated. Studies indicate that loving parents who withhold overt acts of love until misbehavior is corrected have children who develop into young people who are self-disciplined and able to handle the decisions of life.

Three patterns of discipline are recommended: (1) reward acceptable behavior; (2) withhold approval by suspending rewards or by ignoring the behavior when it is indicative of a transitional stage that will be outgrown; and (3) give disapproval that involves discipline administered to forestall more deviant behavior in the future.

Wisdom is needed in administering balanced discipline. Therefore, ground rules must be established.

(1) Rules should be *reasonable*. This can be established by family discussions in which the guidelines for living are discussed and a consensus is achieved for what are to be the limits of approved behavior.

(2) Rules need to be *communicated* in the language of the child. What is understood by the 10-year-old may not have meaning for the 4-year-old. As children grow, the rules need to be revised according to their ability to understand and the latitude for independence they have earned by demonstrating cooperative behavior.

(3) Rules should be *consistently enforced*. The first infraction should be dealt with summarily. To threaten, nag, or recant is only to lead the child into the insecurity of not knowing where his limits are. Young personalities cry out to know the limits of their liberty. Loving parents are obligated to draw the lines fairly, clearly, and consistently.

On the other hand, parents should reserve the right to make exceptions. These arise when children negotiate beforehand for exceptions, such as coming in at a later hour than usual because of attending an approved activity that will not conclude before the usual curfew hour.

For instance, a family has a curfew of 11 o'clock. If the teenager is to be at a service or activity that does not conclude until 11, he cannot be home at 11 also. Time must be allowed for getting home from the place of the activity. When these exceptions are planned and everyone is informed, harmony is maintained and the flexibility that draws out trusting behavior can be demonstrated.

Spare the Rod

A lot has been said about sparing the rod and spoiling the child. So much so, that some parents have taken the idea that the rod or corporal punishment is required for all transgressions. Actually, the method of discipline should be in keeping with the offense. Many times the withholding of privileges is more effective than physical punishment.

A study of the use of the word *rod* in the Old Testament is helpful. The first use of *rod* is that of the scepter or rod of *authority* used to symbolize the position of the father as head of the clan (Psalm 23:4). In this sense, the "rod" is the God-given leadership role the father has in the Christian home (Ephesians 5:23; 6:4). It is his privilege and responsibility to establish a code of honor that marks the value system of the home, proclaiming that Christ is Lord of all.

The second use of "rod" is the counting stick used to separate the sheep to make sure each one was accounted for. Remember the story of the shepherd counting only 99 sheep? He went out into the storm to find the one that was lost (Luke 15:3-7). Parental

38

accountability is a vital use of the "rod" in the Christian family. It implies knowing where the children are and being interested in their comings and goings.

Third, the "rod" was used as a *weapon* on the lion and bear that attacked the flock. Note: the "rod" was not intended for use against the sheep—only those forces that would attack the sheep. Solomon did allow, however, when a child begins to act more like the lion, the bear, or the devil, instead of the sheep, the rod could be applied in chastisement as a deterrent from further deterioration toward rebellion (Proverbs 10:14; 13:24; 22:15; 23:13, 14). The hope is that the child will see the error of his ways and correct his conduct (Hebrews 12:6-13). For rebellion is as the sin of witchcraft (1 Samuel 15:22, 23).

If discipline is discipling, then, example and correction should be balanced in the Christian home. Discipline that is corrective must be administered in keeping with the seriousness of the rule infraction. A variety of approaches will need to be used to reinforce the kind of behavior that is appropriate in the Christian home.

Individual Differences

What works with one child may not work with another. Parents must be alert to individual differences when it comes to meeting the needs of children in establishing disciplined behavior. Whereas one child may respond to a glance, another will respond to the tone of voice, and another may have to feel the pressure of adult hands. Effective parenting requires that parents become sensitive to the individual needs of each child and respond accordingly.

One teenager said to her mother, "I know you are trying to be a good mother, but you are making a dreadful mistake. You are trying to treat all three of us alike. I just happen to need more love than the other two."

Insight into the individual needs of each child in the Christian family helps parents gauge the kind of attention each child needs. More often than not, positive reinforcement will be more effective than physical punishment.

After all, Christian parents do not punish their children. Punishment is reserved as retribution for committed sin. Only God punishes—and He punishes only the sinner. Discipline, however, is the kind of correction that a loving parent administers to get the child's attention before his behavior deviates too far from the accepted path. Don't forget the value of the Word as preventive discipline (2 Timothy 3:16, 17).

The parents' secret tool in becoming aware of individual differences is *listening.* Parents frequently talk too much. They talk when they should be listening to their children. It is amazing how much can be learned about the things that are buzzing around in young minds when adults listen to what their children are saying—both by their words and their actions (body language).

Parental listening should be creative—listening to what the children are saying, not what the parents assume they are saying or what they want to know. This is the application of Deuteronomy 6:7 in the Christian home. It is listening, sharing, and teaching through table talk, while working together around the house, at bedtime, and in the morning while preparing for the day's activities.

Encouraging Self-Discipline

The progress of developing self-discipline—the introduction of control into the life of a child—is in three stages.

Compliance or conformity to family expectations begins as children are taught what is expected of them and given positive reinforcement to encourage their cooperation in meeting expectations. The child's initial motive may be conformity to avoid the problems that arise from disobedience—discipline, correction, reproof. As love in the home develops, the motive matures to please the parent who is admired as an example of a better way to respond.

Identification comes about when the child admires the parents and wants to be like them. This begins deliberately but becomes unconscious as the life-style of the respected elders becomes personally meaningful. The child so admires his adult models that he becomes like them without actually trying.

Internalization follows. This occurs when behavior is so personally meaningful to the child that he no longer cooperates just to keep peace or harmony—or even because of personal admiration for respected elders. The behavior becomes spontaneous because it has become a part of his inner developing personality.

Internalization is the process of making values personal. Modeling will have completed its work in young lives when internal controls operate when the children are away from their parents. This is evidenced in boys and girls whose conduct away from home or behind the back of their parents is as exemplary or more so than when they are with them.

"Behind the scenes" behavior is the real test of obedience—when it is demonstrated spontaneously with no one around to make a record of it or to reward it.

Discipline in the Christian home begins with self-disciplined parents who demonstrate the higher forms of consistent Christian living in such a way that the Christ life becomes the desired behavior and young lives follow their parents in identifying with the claims of Christ on their own lives (Galatians 2:20; 1 Corinthians 11:1).

The hymn writer has put it:

Trust and obey,
For there's no other way
To be happy in Jesus,
But to trust and obey.

When parents adopt this attitude as their guide in responding to spiritual opportunities and responsibilities, they give their children the kind of example needed to internalize spiritual controls. The result is consistent Christian behavior in and out of the home that testifies to His lordship in the life of each member of the family.

CHAPTER FIVE
Reaching Out

IN EXAMINING WHAT IT MEANS to love your neighbor as yourself, we have already examined what this means in the husband-wife and parent-child relationship. We have seen that loving God adequately in a vertical relationship is the beginning of stabilizing family relationships on the horizontal plane. This horizontal dimension of "neighbor" love moves beyond loving members of the immediate and extended families into the fellowship of believers and ultimately emcompasses the whole world.

Immediate Family

The first institution God created was the family. It is still His primary concern. Problems arose early in history. Murder developed in the heart of the first natural-born sons of the human race (Genesis 4:1-15). Since then, Cain's question has been echoed throughout history, "Am I my brother's keeper?" God's answer is, "Yes!"

Sibling rivalry is the name given to friction between children of the same parents. The Bible is replete with examples of sibling rivalry that fragmented relationships. Animosities between Jacob and Esau (Genesis 27), Joseph and his brothers (Genesis 37), and the sons of David (1 Kings 1) are only samples of the problems that come into the home when all is not well between members of the immediate family.

Further problems come when there is friction between parents and children, such as between David and Absalom (2 Samuel 18), Isaac and Jacob (Genesis 27), and Eli and his sons (1 Samuel 2:22-25; 3:11-14; 4:4-18).

On the other hand, relationships are harmonious when the love of God is expressed. The positive parent-child relationships of Jochebed and Moses (Exodus 2:1-9), Hannah and Samuel (1 Samuel 2:1-21), Jephthah and his daughter (Judges 11:30-40), and Jesus and His mother (Luke 2:51, 52; John 2:3-5; 19:26, 27) show loving concern under trying circumstances. Paul highlights the strength of loving influence to the third generation in referring to the relationship of Timothy to his mother Eunice and grandmother Lois (2 Timothy 1:5).

Among brothers, the interaction of creative love is illustrated in the lives of Andrew and Peter (John 1:40-42), James and John (Matthew 4:21, 22), and Judah and Benjamin (Genesis 44).

Extended Family

As the first family grew, the extended family came into being. By the time of Adam's death, seven generations had been born. Using the chronology of the line of Seth in Genesis 5, Adam was still alive when his great-great-great-great-great grandson Methuselah was born. All of the firstborn sons of each generation in between were still alive, plus the "other sons and daughters" of each generation. The population explosion was well on its way! In addition, the descendants of Cain were also proliferating

44

and establishing the first vestiges of civilization as we know it today (Genesis 4:19-22).

Problems arose early in the human history of extended relationships. Friction between the servants of Abraham and Lot led to a parting of the ways for the famous uncle-nephew pair (Genesis 13). In-law relationships pose another area of concern for the extended family. Laban and his son-in-law Jacob (Genesis 31) had their problems, as did Miriam and Aaron with one of Moses' wives (Numbers 12).

More positive family interaction is seen on the cousin level with Mary and Elisabeth (Luke 1:39-58) and with Mordecai and Esther (Esther 2; 4). One only has to turn to the story of Ruth and Naomi (Ruth 1) and Moses and Jethro (Exodus 18) to see how positive in-law interaction can be.

Cultivating an appreciation for members of the extended family smooths human relationships and allows the Spirit to make Christian-family interaction an example of harmony to the world community.

Church Family

Within the fellowship of believers, Christians have the unique honor of being children of God, sons and daughters of the same Heavenly Father, and joint-heirs with Jesus Christ (Romans 8:14-17). In this relationship we are admonished by God's Word to let brotherly love continue (Hebrews 13:1) and to love one another (John 15:12, 17; 1 John 3:11; 2 John 5).

It is in loving each other as brothers and sisters in Christ that we experience the deepest filial relationships possible. Such Christian love transcends human love and prepares us for the interaction that leads from this life into the life to come.

A recent illustration of the depth of Christian brotherhood comes from Nigeria. During the Biafran civil war, the believers were forced to flee to the jungles for survival. Instead of running as individuals or clans, the Christians banded together as church congregations and retreated together, taking their pastor with them.

Everywhere they went they established new congregations and built churches. When the war was over and the Christians were free to return to their original homes, they left churches everywhere they had stopped in flight. Today the new churches are thriving and the old churches have been reestablished. The result: twice as many congregations with a healthy awareness of what it means to share in Christian love, physical survival, and evangelistic witnessing.

Tracing the travels of Paul across the pages of the New Testament reveals the vitality of a Christian faith in new settings and difficult places. The universal family of believers is admonished to share in Christian love and service, recognizing the sovereignty of the universal Father.

Community Relationships

Another dimension of concern as Christian love reaches farther out from the immediate family is the world community. This encompasses the lost world of men and women of every nationality, race, language, and ethnic group.

When Jesus commanded His followers to love their neighbors as themselves, He included all men everywhere. There are neither geographical nor ethnic limits to the extent of the Great Commission (Matthew 28:19). To accomplish the intent of Christ in world evangelism requires each Christian to see the lost as brothers, not strangers. It is only as brotherly love reaches out to encompass the lost that the full scope of Christian brotherhood will be achieved and the coming of the Lord be brought nearer.

But, as Jesus made clear, this concept of brotherhood must begin at home and move in concentric circles until it envelops the world (Acts 1:8). Starting with the four walls we call home, the Word instructs us to be concerned about the welfare of those in our immediate household, the extended family, and the neighbors on our block and in our community, until our concern encompasses the entire globe. As illustrated in the story of the Good Samaritan, "neighbor" includes all whose paths cross ours, giving us an opportunity to reach out and touch them for the sake of the kingdom of heaven (Luke 10:25-37).

Community concern is taught in the family by parents who demonstrate their interest in others by example. Acts of kindness, thoughtfulness, and consideration to others give the example to young lives of the kind of concern that illustrates the practical aspects of brotherly love. The helping, sharing personality is not only more normal, it is more attractive. Such illustrations on the part of parents and significant others in the life of a child are essential in teaching brotherly love as God intended.

The Stewardship of Love

Becoming the kind of loving person who can reach out and touch human lives requires taking inventory of what one has to offer. This encompasses Christian stewardship.

It takes *time* to reach out in Christian love to touch the lives of others. With the busyness of life in the 20th century, it is easy to put off until a more convenient time active intervention in the lives of others to show them the depth of Christian concern. It is never easy; it is never convenient.

To love your neighbor in the way the Lord wants you to requires ordering priorities so time will be planned in the regular schedule of life to touch others so their lives may be enhanced by your deliberate intervention to share with them the influence of a Christ-motivated life.

It also takes *energy*. You cannot reach out to tourch others without getting involved. It is easy to find excuses for noninvolvement, which is one of the social ills of our time. Christian love requires vulnerability, the exposing of yourself to others in time and energy so that Christian witness occurs. Involvement is not always easy, but love is long-suffering and extends itself to meet human need.

Trust is involved in reaching out. This is first trusting ourselves enough to care; then, trusting others enough to share. It is in laying aside momentarily the clamor of our immediate needs to be aware of the needs of others that we broaden our perspective of human need. The trusting person who demonstrates faith in others is a sterling demonstration of what it means to be his "brother's keeper," one who loves his neighbor as himself.

The Christian who cares demonstrates active *concern* for the welfare of others. It is not doing to receive, but rather doing for no other reason than caring as a brother in Christ. Since the spiritual brotherhood supersedes natural family ties, the creative concern of a Christian for others will be demonstrated in the household of faith.

Such a closeness in Christ is novel in many cultures where blood ties are the essence of life. The culture of the Kingdom, however, requires that the spiritual family be seen in an exalted position and that all relationships be cultivated in light of eternal values.

In reaching out to others, whether in your immediate family, extended family, church family, or the world community, the priority is in loving each other on a spiritual level as a basis for testimony and witness to unify believers in Christ and introduce the lost to the values of the kingdom of heaven.

A final dimension in the stewardship of love is *selflessness*. No conditions are imposed on the loved one. No attempt is made to get others to conform to individual expectations. Rather, the loving one is sensitive to the needs of others and shares because of his Christian concern. Such love is not possessive, but allows the other to be free to develop, according to his own abilities, a life that will honor Christ and His kingdom. The honesty of such love negates any attempt to exploit or manipulate another, but seeks only to bring out the good that is being cultivated by the Spirit of Christ in the life of the one loved.

Back to the Model

To love as Christ wants the believer to love—in his own family and the family of God—it is necessary to get back to the model. How much did Christ love the Church? To the point of death, the ultimate sacrifice (Ephesians 5:25-27).

Christ is not telling the Christian of today that he must lay down his life for his friend, brother, or

49

neighbor (John 15:13). However, He is saying that it may be necessary to give generously of time, energy, and self if the ties that bind believers are to be eternally strong.

The more we study God's Word and examine the life of Christ, the more indicators we find that help us identify with the values of Christ and exemplify the thought patterns that motivated Him to lead a life totally submissive to God's will (Philippians 2:5-8). *The Living Bible's* paraphrase of the first verse is enlightening: "Your attitude should be the kind that was shown us by Jesus Christ."

An attitude is a relatively enduring tendency to respond consistently with feeling to beliefs that have been learned through experience with people, places, objects, ideas, and concepts. Attitudes represent the stance or behavioral position a person takes toward the forces that strike him.

How do you view your position in the family? How do you view your relationship on the job or in the community? In reaching out to love others as God wants us to on the horizontal level, it is important to be aware of the attitudes that motivate us to do the things we do—and leave out the things we do not do.

Ever notice how plants bend in the direction of their light source? Why? Light is the source of their strength. Plants left too long by a sunny window have a way of bending into the light. So it is with the Christian personality. It bends in the direction of its energy source. So Paul is saying, let the bend, direction, or attitude of your life demonstrate that you are learning in the direction of Christ as your energy source.

Attitudes are relatively enduring. They become resistant to change with age and experience. So, the older we grow, the less flexible we become. It is important to inculcate the attitudes of Christ in young lives so they can see the example of gracious Christian living and seek to emulate the models they see on display (1 Corinthians 11:1; Philippians 3:17; 1 Thessalonians 1:5-7; 1 Peter 5:1-3).

Another aspect of attitudes is significant to the Christian: attitudes cannot be measured, they are inferred from behavior. Since there is no way to measure what is going on in the human mind, the only indication that can be drawn is from behavioral demonstration. At this point, actions speak louder than words. What the believer thinks is demonstrated in his everyday life.

It is in thinking as Christ thought that we learn to live as He wants to live through us in the present generation. It is letting Him live through us in strengthening human relationships that we know the excitement of being united with Him in loving our brother and neighbor as ourselves.

CHAPTER SIX

Love in a New Dimension

The Spectrum of Love

ALMOST A CENTURY AGO (1883) Henry Drummond delivered a lecture in Central Africa entitled "The Greatest Thing in the World." He was referring to love as illustrated in 1 Corinthians 13. As a scientist, Drummond drew an analogy between love and light. "Light is something more than the sum of its ingredients—a glowing, dazzling, tremulous ether. And love is something more than all of its elements—a palpitating, quivering, sensitive, living thing."

As a prism breaks down a shaft of light into the colors of the rainbow, so Paul breaks down the dimensions of love into nine component parts, each representing a different aspect of love that blends into the wholeness of loving behavior.

Love eludes definition. Through the centuries, however, writers have tried to describe it. To Montaigne, love was "an insatiate thirst for enjoying a greedily desired object." Henry Van Dyke, however, saw love as "the heart's immortal thirst to be completely known and all forgiven." In the view of Ben Jonson, love was "a spiritual coupling of two souls," whereas Bellinghausen saw it as "two souls with a single thought, two hearts that beat as one."

Paul's description of love in nine facets is the most beautiful in literature. Each aspect has a special meaning when applied to the loving behavior that permeates Christian home and family living.

Patience

"Love suffereth long" Drummond sees as "love passive, love waiting to begin; not in a hurry; calm; ready to do its work when the summons comes but meantime wearing the ornament of a meek and quiet spirit."

The patience of love shows itself in putting no limiting restrictions on the loved one. Trying to press another person into the mold of preconceived ideas is the antithesis of loving behavior.

To grow, each member of the Christian family must have freedom to develop in his own unique way. There are role expectations on us all. There are role expectations for the male and another set for the female; one set for adults and another for children. Love takes the cultural expectations and allows individual differences to emerge, so each can develop honestly the aptitudes he has and the interests that are unique to his personality.

A love that understands and waits becomes tolerant of time and space. It is love passive, waiting for fulfillment, not chafing under the delay of gratification.

Kindness

Love that is kind seeks to give pleasure spontaneously without ulterior motive. It looks for the gestures and tones in conversation that will put the best light on discussions.

Kindness does not probe. It does not insist on answers before they can be given. Nor does it contrive situations that will put a loved one on the spot.

The kindness of love does not point out the inefficiencies of another. It never questions courage, integrity, or strength. Rather, it seeks ways to be supportive. Those who work outside the home are being shown their inferiorities repeatedly. At home they need reassurance. They need to know that in the sanctity of the Christian home there are those who take them as they are—imperfections and all—and accept them without recrimination.

Kindness looks for the little ways in which to express joy and appreciation: a touch of the hand, a word of appreciation, a thoughtful gesture. Such considerations need not wait for holidays or anniversaries. They are appropriate any time in the home where kindness is a spontaneous demonstration of love.

Kindness is love aggressive—seeking ways to enhance loving relationships and bolstering the confidences that lead to spontaneity.

Generosity

The love that "envieth not" is the kind that is not jealous. Most jealousy in the Christian family centers on persons, time, energy, or accomplishments. Rather than being jealous of others, the way they spend their time and energy, or the accomplishments they achieve, the generosity of love allows each member of the household to excel in his unique talents and to take the time and energy necessary for fulfillment.

Actually, there are only two reasons for jealousy: history or projection. In history, you know enough about the other person to know from past experience he cannot be trusted, so you work on previous knowledge and let jealousy emerge. In projection, the problem lies within the jealous person. He knows enough about himself to know that in a given situation he could not be trusted, so he projects his own uneasiness on the other and then assumes guilt.

There is no need for jealousy in Christian relationships. When each member of the relationship conducts his life as unto the Lord, there is no history to dig up and no experience from which to project jealousy.

To avoid jealousy and develop generosity in loving behavior, Drummond says it is necessary to be "fortified with the grace of magnanimity. And then, having learned that, you have to learn this further thing, *humility*—to put a seal upon your lips and forget what you have done."

Humility

The "love that vaunteth not itself, is not puffed up" is openly transparent. It waives self-satisfaction in an attempt to let others increase without demanding its own rights.

The humility of love forgets what it has done for the loved one. It acts voluntarily without thought of reward. It is what it is because of the spontaneous outflow of love that is the motivation behind loving behavior. This love quickly notices what others do as loving behavior and is quick to respond appreciatively.

The humility in love realizes that it is more blessed to give than to receive and takes advantage of opportunities to be a helping, sharing person. While not drawing attention to itself, the humility of love can accept without shame the appreciation that comes from others whose welfare has been served selflessly. The humility of love does what is not only right but also appropriate, and then acknowledges it has done so without pride or false humility.

It is through the dimension of humility that love is more honest, admitting, "I did that because I wanted to. I love you."

Courtesy

Courtesy refers to "love in relation to etiquette," love in little things. Drummond observes: "Love cannot behave itself unseemly. You can put the most untutored persons into the highest society, and if they have a reservoir of love in their hearts, they will not behave themselves unseemly. They simply cannot do it."

The courtesy of love is alert to how the loved one views a situation and seeks to bring out the best of every opportunity. There is a vigilance in the courtesy of love, for it is constantly on best behavior because it chooses not to put the loved one on the spot.

Love seeks to know what is correct in a variety of situations and then diligently carries out the appropriate behavior. In so doing, it never embarrasses or lets the relationship appear in a negative light. It is alert to opportunities to do what is right because of a spontaneous desire to stimulate correctness around it. It studies what is right and then seeks to demonstrate it at every opportunity, for love "doth not behave itself unseemly."

Unselfishness

A love that "seeketh not her own" looks intently at what is best for the loved one. It has discovered that "there is no greatness in *things . . . there is no happiness in having, or in getting, but only in giving.*"

In romance, the unselfishness of love seeks what is best for the loved one, no matter what the personal sacrifice. This frequently demands delay of gratification, postponement of immediate rewards for long-range values. In professional choice, it allows the loved one the time, space, and emotional freedom to make adequate preparations to be eligible for admission to and advancement in a chosen field.

In marriage, unselfishness requires preparing adequately for the responsibilities of home and family before expecting to enjoy the benefits of the relationship. Such long-range planning allows all concerned to prepare adequately for their unique responsibilities in the new relationship.

This unselfishness also allows the young to find their own place in life. It helps parents untie the apron string by letting young people make their own choices as to college, courses, and career. Unselfishness does not seek to relive unfulfilled ambitions through the young, but allows them the freedom of moving toward their own goals as they become aware of their strengths and weaknesses in relation to long-range ambitions.

Self-control

A good temperament "is not easily provoked." This part of love speaks to emotional maturity, the ability to know the motive behind behavior. Each person has his own "boiling point," that level of pressure that leads to unanticipated behaviors.

The good temper of love demonstrates self-control which, in turn, has its origin in an adequate self-concept. This involves being agent of one's own responses and responsible for one's own actions.

Lack of self-control can show itself in a variety of reactions which run the gamut from depression to unrestrained activity. Love seeks a balance between extremes, yet keeps an activity level that is spontaneously stimulating. It steers a course between overrestrictive control and unrestrained expression.

The concept that love is revealed in self-control brings together the previous dimensions of the attitude. "For a want of patience, a want of courtesy, a want of unselfishness, are all instantaneously symbolized in one flash of temper." That which is precious and the product of tedious cultivation can be dashed in an unrestrained moment. It takes longer to rekindle a flame that has been extinguished by a flash of temper than it takes to ignite it in the first place.

Love that is to last a lifetime must have a generous supply of self-control.

Guilelessness

The love that "thinketh no evil" imputes no motive to the actions of others. Drummond points out that "the people who influence you are people who believe in you." We need to be surrounded by people who cultivate an atmosphere of encouragement around us. This aspect of love puts only the best connotation on actions. It demonstrates the absence of fear, anger, hate, and lust, the negative emotions that fragment relationships.

Going a step deeper, this concept of love is also forgiving. It not only imputes no motive to behavior, but when it discovers that it has been betrayed, love comes through with forgiveness that keeps no record of wrongs and extracts no punitive penalty.

This aspect of love lets the parent discipline the child by rejecting behavior without rejecting the child. It allows young lovers to work out their misunderstandings by listening to all the facts before rendering a decision. And, it cultivates positive behavior by anticipating only the highest forms of action.

Sincerity

Pulling the dimensions of love together neatly is the sincerity that runs through the fabric of the relationship. For, love "rejoiceth not in iniquity but rejoiceth in the truth." This is the self-restraint that does not take advantage of the faults or weaknesses of the loved one. Even when it recognizes weaknesses, it does not keep pointing them out either to the loved one or to others.

Love seeks to bring out the strengths and to cultivate the virtues of others. It keeps expecting the strengths to outweigh the weaknesses and gives ample opportunity for right to win.

Sincerity, according to Drummond, includes "the self-restraint which refuses to make capital out of others' faults." It endeavors to see things as they are, not as suspicion would fear them to be.

The meaning behind the word *sincerity* is "without wax." It goes back to the days of marble carving.

Should a sculptor be a shoddy workman and gouge the marble rather than carve it smoothly, he would use wax to cover up the blemish and try to sell the product as perfect. Traders would use their thumbnails to examine a carving closely to make sure there was no wax worked into the object.

In the sincerity of love there is no wax, no fill-in, no cover-up. There is open, transparent communication that leaves no room for flaws to be camouflaged. Nothing is deliberately held back that could later show a crack in the artistic relationship developing through maturing love.

The contemporary meaning of love in a new dimension—love as Christ wants us to experience it in the Christian family—is best illustrated in the paraphrase of *The Living Bible*: "Love is very patient and kind, never jealous or envious, never boastful or proud, never haughty or selfish or rude. Love does not demand its own way. It is not irritable or touchy. It does not hold grudges and will hardly even notice when others do it wrong. It is never glad about injustice, but rejoices whenever truth wins out. If you love someone you will be loyal to him no matter what the cost. You will always believe in him, always expect the best of him, and always stand your ground in defending him" (1 Corinthians 13:4-7).

When all else fails, love survives. The three most permanent elements of relationships are faith, hope, and love. Of these, Paul says, the greatest and most enduring is love (v. 13).

CHAPTER SEVEN

Aggressive Love

Kinds of Love

LOVE IS MORE THAN SINKING INTO HIS ARMS and ending up with your arms in the sink. True, love means different things to different people. Three words are used in the Greek to differentiate among the dimensions of love, the *charity,* of 1 Corinthians 13.

Eros does not appear in the Bible but appears frequently in classical Greek literature. It is associated with the erotic and sensuous. Pornography in art and literature caters to this type of stimulation. The emphasis is on sexual fulfillment as reduction of a biological need, not the social or spiritual qualities of a relationship. In marriage, *eros* refers to the physical side of lovemaking and is a legitimate and valued part of the relationship.

Phileo is brotherly love, a fondness for a person, even a family pet. It comes from a Greek word that implies affection and personal attachment involving sentiment and feeling. The word for Philadelphia, meaning "city of brotherly love," comes from this Greek word. Love on this basis is more emotional, inconsistent, and changeable. It involves mental assent more than commitment and does not carry the depth of spiritual qualities implied in the attitudes of love in 1 Corinthians 13.

Agape is the highest form of love. It has a spiritual quality to it. When the New Testament was written, *agape* was a relatively new word in the Greek language. It means to love with all the heart—the heart being interpreted in the first century as the seat of affection. It is this highest form of love that is used consistently in 1 Corinthians 13, and the kind of love that illustrates an enduring, mature attitude toward a loved person.

In Christian marriage, love must be demonstrated as well as professed. Love that is worthy of a Christian couple involves *empathy* for the loved one. This is the ability to feel as the loved one feels, to share his emotions, sorrows, disappointments, joys, and quiet times.

True love also involves a deep *concern* for the welfare, happiness, and development of the loved one as a person. This love recognizes the needs of the loved one and allows him the freedom to develop his own strengths, interests, and abilities in accordance with the uniqueness of his own personality. It offers opportunity for fulfillment to become what the loved one believes under Christ he is capable of becoming.

In addition, worthy love finds *pleasure* in making his own resources available to the loved one. This includes strength, time, energy, money, intelligence, and creativity. A person who really loves is not only concerned about the welfare and development of the one he loves. He does something positive about it.

Fragmenting Love

Some behaviors that emerge in the dating scene are called love when they are more a display of *infatuation*. Infatuation comes suddenly and looks only on the parts of personality that are compatible with immediate expectations. It is centered in self and based more on wishful thinking, even fantasy, than reality. It becomes demanding and physical in nature, to the point of being compulsive. Unfortunately, it changes suddenly and is highly unpredictable.

When infatuation is taken for love, it leads to frustration. That is why it is appropriate to say that love is an attitude that grows as a result of a relationship; it is not a cause to begin one.

Conditional love, for instance, is a kind of relationship that says, "I will do this for you if you will do this other thing for me." It is based on bargaining and is never satisfied because it keeps raising the demand of conformity (Judges 16:4-19).

Possessive love, on the other hand, encourages the treatment of another personality as private property. It does not allow the freedom that is necessary to develop independently. As a result, it leads to the "clinging vine" syndrome that ceases to grow into a mature relationship (2 Samuel 11:2-27).

Romanticized love maintains a constant display of adoration and excitement, almost to the point of idolatry. It is so idealized that it would be impossible for any flesh-and-blood individual to live up to its expectations. When the glamor has worn off, the flame of worship ceases to burn (1 Samuel 18:20, 21; 2 Samuel 6:16).

Deceitful love is probably the most devastating charade that love takes. One person professes to love the other and then takes advantage of him for selfish purposes. This kind of love for gratification exploits and is devastating to a long-term relationship (Genesis 27).

Insecure love grows out of a need for security. Feeling inadequate, a lover reaches out to grasp an object for personal reinforcement. This kind of love is seen in teenage marriages when youth choose marriage as an escape from home, school, job, or other confrontations with maturity.

Mutually destructive love is a kind of neurotic relationship in which each partner drains emotional strength from or tears down the other. This kind of love sooner or later turns more into hate than into real love.

Two-against-the-world love is the kind of destructive relationship that emerges when marriage partners band together against their families to establish a marriage. Then, when the families accept the choice of the couple and stop fighting their planned togetherness, there is nothing cohesive to hold them together. They banded together against pressure, but have nothing to sustain them when the pressure is off.

These forms of attraction, mistakenly called love, are common in the world today but are inferior as a basis for a Christ-centered relationship.

Mix in Marriage

Differences between marriage partners, beyond their maleness or femaleness and masculinity or femininity, add up to what is called *mix* in marriage. Gross differences in such areas as age, race, education, nationality, social and economic status, and religion are the factors that contribute to mix in marriage. The only one of these mixes to which the Bible speaks specifically is religious mix. The others are sociological problems.

Peter proclaimed that marriage need not be a hindrance to spirituality, nor should it interfere with Christian service (1 Peter 3:1-7). It is true that compatibility in religious attitudes within marriage lends stability to the relationship. That is why Paul encouraged believers to marry within the faith and not be unequally yoked together with unbelievers (2 Corinthians 6:14).

To the wife who becomes a Christian after her marriage but whose husband has not joined her on a spiritual quest, Peter has some sound suggestions. Certainly the apostle did not see this mix in marriage as grounds for interrupting the relationship. In fact, both Peter and Paul stressed that incompatibility of religious views did not justify dissolution of marriage. Rather, this is an opportunity to let the graces and disciplines of the Christ life show in the marriage as a witness to the unbeliever (1 Corinthians 7:12-16). Don't leave him, Paul says—win him!

The Irresistible Woman

The irresistible woman, according to Peter, is the one whose consistent Christian life-style is a challenge to her husband and draws his attention to the beauty of a consistent Christian example.

"Word" in 1 Peter 3:1 refers to the Word of God, the Bible. "Conversation" refers to the consistent life-style of the believing woman. And "won" suggests that the unbelieving husband will be inspired to turn to Christ because of the virtues and graces of his godly wife. The "fear" of verse 2 is reverence or awe that is inspired by a consistent walk with Christ and respect for her husband, not the cringing fear that stifles emotional growth (Ephesians 5:33).

Peter is saying, in modern English: "If any obey not God's Word, they also may without nagging about the Bible be won by the consistent life-style of the wife whose daily demonstration of faith is marked by reverence for God and respect for her husband." Or, as *The Living Bible* paraphrases it: "Wives, fit in with your husbands' plans; for then if they refuse to listen when you talk to them about the Lord, they will be won by your respectful, pure behavior. Your godly lives will speak to them better than any words."

Adorning is a key word in this passage (v. 3). Peter points out that the kind of costume, cosmetics, and jewelry some women use to attract men may not necessarily win a man to Christ. Simply, being seductive is not an evangelism technique. For attire designed to stimulate the physical nature of a man conflicts with the loftiest spiritual ideals.

Such a warning is again appropriate when an emphasis on sexuality and seductiveness is being promulgated in some circles as a phase of evangelism. Sexiness is not necessarily conducive to evangelism. In many cases it only clouds the issue and distracts from the intent of the gospel message. This in no way implies that the "beautiful Christian" is not also a cooperative partner in marriage, but the emphasis is not on the physical but rather on the spiritual.

The word *kosmos* is used in the original text to suggest that the adorning of the irresistible woman is orderly, the opposite of *chaos*. Adorning in style, cut, color, and design should be an ordered system in keeping with the body structure of the virtuous woman. Her attire should be fitting, congruous, with her body style, and not diverse from her character or garish.

The problem arises when a woman professes to be a Christian but is adorned as a woman of the world; basically calling the attention of men other than her husband to her body rather than her disciplined spirit.

The character of the irresistible woman is described as meek and of a quiet spirit. It is interesting that the only word description we have of Jesus is the one in which He calls himself "meek and lowly" (Matthew 11:29). In the Beatitudes, it is the meek who inherit the earth (Matthew 5:5). They do not work for it or earn it, they inherit it as a privilege of their personal relationship with Christ. Such is the irresistible woman who wins her husband to Christ and testifies by a consistent life-style to the members of her own household.

"Amazement" arises in the text to remind the Christian wife that if she is living before her husband as Christ wants her to, she will never have to fear being caught in a compromising situation (1 Peter 3:6). She does not have to fear the knock on the door or the ringing of the telephone. At all times her Spirit-controlled life is in keeping with her husband's expectations of her.

The Deserving Man

What kind of man deserves this special kind of woman? Peter is assuming that the testimony of the woman described early in this chapter will bring her husband to a knowledge of Christ. For, in verse 7 the husband is a believer. He is encouraged to bring all of his cognitive powers to bear on their relationship.

He is instructed to demonstrate an intelligent recognition of the responsibilities of marriage as well as its privileges.

"Honor" in this verse is translated "precious" in 1 Peter 1:19. Only God and a Christian gentleman know the value of a virtuous woman. It is his privilege to treat her as a treasured object. The "weaker vessel" in this passage is not Peter's attempt to picture the wife as inferior. Rather, he is suggesting that she is beautiful, special, fragile—like crystal.

What woman serves breakfast every morning on her crystal? No, she keeps the crystal for those special occasions—such as candlelight dinners—but uses pottery, plastic, or ironstone for everyday use. So Peter sees the wife not as a vessel for the convenience of a man but rather as an object of worth reserved for special occasions. Why? Because they both—the deserving husband and his irresistible wife—are joint-heirs with Jesus Christ, children of the same Father (Romans 8:17).

Then Peter makes a practical observation. Bickering between husband and wife hinders the efficacy of family prayers. When there is strife between the couple and lack of honor between the husband and wife, the spiritual vitality of the home is hampered. The first place to look for the effect of this tension is in unanswered prayer.

Are your prayers going unanswered? Do you find your spiritual tide at a low ebb? Look at the quality of communication between husband and wife. If due honor and reverence is being demonstrated, the way is open through prayer to tap the resources of the kingdom of heaven, for the meek inherit the earth now in anticipation of eternity to come.

The Compatible Couple

The compatible couple evaluates their motivation for marriage. They recognize the intellectual, spiritual, social, and physical dimensions of their attraction to each other. They love on the *agape* level but do not deny the *eros* and *phileo* degrees to their physical relationship. Because of this, they are sensitive to the needs of their partner. They do not withhold physical gratification in marriage for selfish reasons. Neither are they selfishly overdemanding. They present themselves to each other because their marriage before Christ gives them the opportunity to express through verbal and body language the depth of love for a partner that has been brought into their lives through a loving Creator God.

Rather than defraud, cheat, or withhold gratification, they participate freely in the physical expressions of loving behavior. The only time they refrain from the sexual expression of their love is for a spiritual fast, and that for a very limited time. Never should withholding of physical expressions of love be prolonged, says Paul, because the devil delights in tempting the sexually deprived and leading them outside of marriage into promiscuous sin (1 Corinthians 7:1-5).

CHAPTER EIGHT
A Christian View of Sexuality

Designed by God

GOD CREATED THE WORLD FOR MAN. When the ecological balance of the universe was stable, God formed man out of the dust of the earth, breathed into him divine life, and man became a living soul (Genesis 1:24-31; 2:19, 20). Adam had the intelligence to name every creature and plant that God had made. He was a thinking, rational being.

God's creation was good. It was beautiful. In this creation was every kind of pleasure man's heart could desire. His aesthetic needs were intrigued by the beauty of nature. The form and movement of God's creation blended together to worship Him in a blaze of perfection. Affection could be expressed with the domestic animals that curried his favor and curled at his feet.

One thing was missing in the original creation, however. There was no creature of equal intelligence and spiritual insight with whom man could share on an intimate level. So God created woman as a companion for man, a creation designed to communicate on every level of man's need (Genesis 2:18).

In chapter 3 we noted that the word *rib* in Genesis 2:21, 22 means "flank," a major portion of Adam's side. Eve was made from the same material already existing in man. She was made to be his counterpart, mirror image, a helper adequate to meet his needs.

This underscores the equality of the husband and wife in a Christian marriage relationship (Galatians 3:28). They were made by the same God from the same material but altered in design just enough to be the "completer" of each other. It takes two to be one flesh in the intimacy of a God-ordained physical relationship (Genesis 2:23-25).

The openness without shame with which Adam viewed his newly created wife is descriptive of the transparent relationship God desires the Christian husband and wife to have on all levels of their relationship—nothing concealed, nothing hidden, nothing between them in their honesty. This is what the sincerity of love in 1 Corinthians 13 is all about.

Meeting the physical needs of each other in the intimacy of Christian marriage is a God-ordained right and one of the pledges inherent in the marriage vows. The relationship is that of celebrating (observing) a spiritual privilege with the blessing of the Lord who so designed His special creation (Hebrews 13:4).

Love and Sex

It is important to distinguish between love and sex. Love is an attitude. As such it is controlled by the parasympathetic nervous system which is activated primarily by the brain. Because of its cognitive relationship, love tolerates time and space and does not clamor for immediate expression.

Viet Nam veterans illustrate a point. When the prisoners of war were being returned, it was anticipated they would need extensive therapy in order to function adequately since they had been deprived of heterosexual fulfillment for so long. This proved to be true only in isolated cases, however. Men who remained true to their wives in loyal love without sexual gratification were able to respond normally as they had before their enforced celibacy. This is just another indication that tolerance of time and space is a quality of love that remains constant in spite of trying circumstances.

Sex, on the other hand, may be viewed as an emotion. As such it is controlled by the sympathetic nervous system, the part that handles the reflexes of survival. Sex as an emotion is possessive, compulsive, and does not tolerate time and space. It is characterized by urgency for immediate gratification.

In moving from love to sex, the nervous system shifts gears. It is understanding this distinction and handling the feelings that go with sex and love that helps the single Christian maintain his sexual purity while anticipating the privileges of Christian marriage. Until this distinction is learned, unnecessary tensions exist in relationships—before and after marriage—that are difficult to handle.

History is replete with illustrations of love without sex—individuals who loved each other but never consummated their love in a physical relationship. History is also strewn with the residue of lives in which sex without love violated human dignity and made violent use of a capacity designed to be held in sacred trust.

So far as sex in Christian marriage is concerned, the axiom is true: it is more blessed to give than to receive. As Erik Erikson has suggested, this requires loving partners of complementary sexes who have determined to share mutual trust and willingness "to regulate the cycles of work, procreation and recreation so as to secure to the offspring, too, all the stages of a satisfactory development."

Love and work must be seen in proper balance so that overwork does not drain energy from the capacity to love and be loved adequately.

Biblical Teachings

The Old Testament consistently sees sex as a gift from God designed for heterosexual relationships within marriage (Genesis 1:26-28; 2:18, 21-25). Sexual activities outside of marriage, however, are listed among the sins that God hates. Among these are extramarital affairs involving both fornication and adultery (Leviticus 20:10). These are pictured as a violation of God's law and an invasion of human dignity.

Singled out for special treatment is incest, sexual relations between members of the immediate family (Leviticus 18:6-18). Not only is this a Biblical sin, it is one of the most universal taboos in anthropology. Most of the tribes, clans, and races of the world have sanctions against parent-child, brother-sister, and other forms of incest.

Particularly deviant from divine design is homosexuality (Leviticus 18:22). This involves male with male (sodomy), which was prevalent in the days of Lot, and female with female (lesbianism), which became an expression of pagan worship in ancient Greece. Especially reprehensible in ancient times was the practice of adult males using young boys as sex partners (pederasty) as a form of birth control, a common custom in the Greece of Socrates and Plato.

The New Testament declares that sex is good in a reaffirmation of Old Testament teachings. Marriage is honorable, the Word declares (Hebrews 13:4). But sexual activity should be restricted to the husband and wife within the bonds of Christian marriage (Matthew 19:4-6). The apostles are united in agreeing that to marry is to agree to cooperate in repetitive cycles of sexual relationships (Ephesians 5:22; 1 Peter 3:1; 1 Corinthians 7:2-4).

On the other hand, sex was never intended to be used as a club or a convenience. Abstinence should only be practiced as a spiritual fast and only when both parties have agreed for a limited time (1 Corinthians 7:5, 6).

In planning the size of their family, a couple should consider the number of children they can provide for adequately. Paul alludes in 1 Timothy 5:8 to a principle that applies here.

The New Testament supports the Old Testament in condemning extramarital relations (Matthew 5:27; 1 Corinthians 6:9, 16-20), incest (1 Corinthians 5:1), fornication (1 Corinthians 6:18), and homosexuality (Romans 1:18-28). Two special classes of homosexuals are noted in 1 Corinthians 6:9: "effeminate" refers to male prostitutes who offer their bodies for lewd practices in pagan worship; and "abusers of themselves" refers to perversions between partners in a homosexual liaison. All of these the Holy Scriptures cry out against as sin.

Sex Through the Centuries

Following the pure teaching of first-century Christianity, the Church began to react against Greek philosophy, the rising Eastern cults, and Western paganism. Virginity and celibacy were exalted as more spiritual states, and restrictions on marriage for those dedicated to Christian service began to appear. It was not so in the beginning, but this did emerge as traditions superseded theology.

By the time of St. Thomas Aquinas and the Scholastics in the Middle Ages, sexual expression was considered a secondary function. Marriage was viewed more as an institution than a personal relationship. The secularization of a primary relationship was almost complete. It was not until the Protestant Reformation, under Martin Luther, that sex was extolled as a legitimate part of Christian marriage. The body is not sinful in itself, he said, sex is as natural as hunger and thirst.

Following the Reformation, fragmentation occurred. The Puritans emphasized complete loyalty to God, implying that this loyalty did not foster positive attitudes toward human sexuality. The Pietists, on the other hand, said that because sex was pleasurable, even within Christian marriage, it must be sinful. Holiness, in their point of view, required denial of sexual pleasure except for procreation. The other extreme was represented by the Rationalists who substituted reason for the authority of Scripture and accepted humanistic morality instead of the purity that comes from God.

As a result of these trends, half truths and distortions about sex increased greatly. Some believe that sex is sin, assuming that the body is evil and its functions nasty. They go so far as to think that sex sins are unforgivable, the worst of sins in God's sight. Further, they proclaim that pleasure is evil, particularly the pleasures derived from sexual expression.

Others would contend that virginity is the only pure state and that the celibate life is holier than married life. Some would allow marriage but proclaim that continence in marriage helps earn favor with God, a direct violation of 1 Corinthians 7:1-6. By analogy, some contend that the first sin was a sexual act between Adam and Eve and that eating the fruit in the Garden is only a figure of speech for it. Another point of view postulates that sexual activity is animal in nature and unworthy of redeemed man, defining sexual desire as a base instinct.

Fortunately, the Word contradicts these teachings. The privilege of the Christian parent is to take an active part in preparing his children with proper attitudes toward human sexuality. Children and young people need to know the truth, the whole truth, but, since sex education is developmental, no more truth than is appropriate for the age and understanding of the child.

From Celibacy to Celebration

Students of human behavior believe that a person, male or female, can go through life without a single sexual orgasm and not suffer physiologically from it. Sex seems to be an appetite that takes on the form of a need with the urgency of a drive. How to respond to this internal chemistry is learned as a result of conditioning in childhood. The strength of this drive varies from time to time, depending on external stimulation as well as internal chemistry. These fluctuations give a person opportunity to monitor his feelings and channel his energies.

Dwight Small in *Christian: Celebrate Your Sexuality* (Old Tappan, NJ: Fleming H. Revell Co., 1974) says:

Sexuality is an expression of the whole person; it belongs to the symphony of human existence. It cannot be compartmentalized, but is the music of the body, complete with rhythms and melodies and harmonies. Throughout the relationship of marriage there plays, as it were, the obbligato of sexual love.

The contemporary society has given a distorted view of sexuality as a positive experience. Small observes:

Our culture has succeeded in squeezing sex into a mold that is too small for it, making it less than the Creator intended it to be. If man's relationship to his own sexuality determines whether he becomes more human or less, then man seemingly is becoming less. The record of our time displays the growing bankruptcy of inner values in our society, and nowhere is this more visible than in our national attitudes toward sex. With greater availability has come greater meaninglessness; this meaninglessness touches all of life, for we are sexual beings, and sexuality is basically the power to relate as persons.

Small is saying it is wrong to think of sex as only a physical response, leaving it on the animal plane.

Redeemed men and women are called upon to make a Christian affirmation of their total being with its multiplied potentials. Small continues on this subject:

Man is infinitely larger than the current theories of human sexuality take him to be. For if human sexuality is less than the mystery of human selfhood—including the mystery of man's relationship to God—then it is less than thoughtful men know it to be. The meaning of sexuality is the meaning of man himself. The Christian affirms that sexuality belongs to the mysteries of divine revelation. In consequence, its ultimate meaning can be known only by revelation. To the non-Christian this is exasperating nonsense, to every committed Christian believer it is fundamental to knowing the truth. . . .

Small quotes from *The Feast of Fools* by Harvey Cox when he says:

Porpoises and chimpanzees may play. Only man celebrates. . . . Celebrative affirmation is "saying yes to life." And this is truly Christian. . . . Whenever the Christian celebrates God's gifts, he is doing so to the glory of God" (1 Corinthians 10:31).

This, according to Small, "includes man's rightful sexual activity." Referring to Romans 12:1, Small suggests:

Spiritual worship includes the offering of one's body and its functioning to God in a veritable sacrifice of living wholly unto Him. Thus does the Christian celebrate. . . . The husband-wife union, is a celebration. Such celebration . . . links us in Christ to the human and divine. That which takes place on the human, bodily plane is elevated in dignity as it is representative of the intimate bond between Christ and His bride, the church of the redeemed . . . Sexuality is God's gift to be received with thanksgiving, offered in faith back to Him in its fulfillment, and celebrated in His holy presence . . . Sexuality is seen as a gift from a bountiful and loving Creator, a gift for man's enjoyment and for the fulfillment of his highest welfare and happiness . . . Only the informed and committed Christian can truly celebrate his sexuality!

CHAPTER NINE

Expectations in Marriage

Masculine Roles

ROLES IN MARRIAGE ARE NOT GAMES people play. They are expectations that have evolved in a culture that both forbids and allows certain behavior. Roles set the limits of some activities and raise the necessity of learning new tasks for others.

A Christian husband, for instance, is the president of a going corporation. At the same time, as a husband, he must be sensitive to the needs of his wife. As a father, he is responsible for training his children in both secular and spiritual pursuits (Proverbs 22: 6). He is an employee and, in some cases, an employer as well. He must be alert to the spiritual demands on his professional life. (Ephesians 6:5, 6, 9; Colossians 3:22, 23).

He is still a son and now a son-in-law. These family relationships must be constantly revised. On the block, he is a neighbor. And, he continues as a relative in the extended family and takes on a new set of extended in-law relationships. These widen the sphere of his influence and broaden the base of his personal considerations (Philippians 2:4). As a citizen, he must be aware of his civic responsibilities and participate in the welfare of his community (1 Timothy 2:1, 3).

Never should the married male lose sight of the fact that he is a Christian worker. In all he says and does, he must be an example to his mate and children of the Christ life and set the pace in participation in spiritual activities. This involves the devotional atmosphere of the home as well as spiritual activities in the church and community (Ephesians 6:4; Proverbs 22:6).

Feminine Roles

Role expectations are as demanding on the Christian wife. She is vice-president of the family corporation (and frequently secretary and treasurer). As a mother she supports the authority of her husband in the home and sets an example of Christian virtue (Titus 2:3-5). There is no higher calling, no more challenging profession than that of Christian motherhood. "Submission to the task of being a wife," say Brandt and Dowdy, "is not the end of freedom, but the beginning of one of the highest and most challenging of professions" (1 Peter 3:1-4; Ephesians 5:22-24, 33).*

As a homemaker, the wife is responsible for the orderliness and organization of the home. Since she spends more hours per week with the children, she has a major input into their education and learning experiences. Should she also choose a career outside the home, she must keep a balance between home and professional involvements so nothing detracts from the quality of the home so far as nurturing the children is concerned. Their earliest years are impressionable, plastic times.

All family activities must be conducted with the welfare of the children in mind. Never should they feel they are in the way or excess baggage on the rocky road of life. The working mother must never neglect the welfare of her children. Quality fathering during this period is essential as well.

The wife continues as a daughter and daughter-in-law with the adjustments entailed by this broadened base of relationships. Her civic responsibilities carry over from her single days. And, her ministry as a Christian worker is unchanged by her marriage. Somehow she must balance the pressures on her time and energy so she can meet the multiple demands.

Territory to Defend

Territory in a marriage is the area of their relationship the husband and wife are willing to defend against outside pressure. For the career-oriented member of the marriage, this involves the profession or vocation and all that entails. It relates to what is necessary to be accepted in a job, to grow in that job, and to find satisfaction in that job.

Many women do not discover it until later, but when a woman marries a man, she marries not only a husband but also a career. A man must find satisfaction in his vocational choice, or dissatisfactions will reduce him to feeling as though he is only half a man. This will have severe repercussions on the marriage unless the self-concept can be rescued.

If the wife is career-oriented, her professional life falls into this area. She also must find fulfillment in her vocational field to compensate for the time she spends outside the home, especially if there are children depending on her care.

From the standpoint of child development, the quality of mothering a child receives in the preschool years is tremendously important for the development of personality and an adequate self-concept. The major contribution parents make in the personality development of their child is made before the child is 8 years old. For this reason, it is essential that the quality of parental time must be at a peak during the early years of the child.

A mother who works because she is vocation-oriented may be able to add quality to the togetherness because of the fulfillment she derives from her career. On the other hand, if she is working because of necessity, the dissatisfactions brought home from the job can be a hindrance to wholesome family interaction. In most cases, it is better for the mother not to work from the time the first child is born until after the last one is in school. The quality of moral and ethical training during these plastic years will determine the direction teenage character will be bent.

An area of overlapping in territory is represented by the children's education. Although the mother usually is closer to the educational program of her children, it is advisable for the father to take an interest in what the children are doing and to be aware of the kinds of people who are influencing the educational life of his children. Attendance at school functions, especially when his children are performing, is important to the psychological development of the child.

Another area of overlapping where the mother and father interact together in defending the territory of the family is in spiritual life. The church and its educational and evangelistic programs need to be integrated into the fabric of the home. What is learned in Sunday school should be discussed at

82

home. The attitudes and values taught in church should be given opportunity for examination and development at home.

One of the best ways to do this is to check the adequacy of the family's devotional life. Although the father, as priest of the household, is responsible for the spiritual life of the home, the mother and father must work together at maintaining family devotions and worship times in the home. It is in sharing in the spiritual vitality of the family that optimal opportunity is given for togetherness in the Christian home. This is one of the unique aspects the Christian home has to offer.

Orbit of Movement

Further removed from the role and territory is the orbit in which family interaction moves. This includes the community activities and civic responsibilities the parents feel are appropriate for the family and for their own personal fulfillment. There are many civic activities in which the husband or wife will be involved alone—civic clubs, organizations, and associations, as well as political and social activities. Others are more related to the vocational and professional involvements.

Even though each may go his own way in the orbit, there needs to be a maximum of overlapping where the family can be involved together. This will include family recreation, hobbies, field trips, vacations, and other extracurricular activities that take the family outside the home into the community and world of normal healthy living.

In this regard it is only right to note that each partner in the marriage should have time and money to use for personal pursuits in which the other may not share. It is essential that this amount be budgeted so that it is not overbalanced in one direction. The confidence of the couple must be such that there are no questions as to the legitimacy of these expenditures. This psychological freedom is essential to maintain individuality and a sense of personal worth which contribute creatively to a healthy marriage relationship.

Identity is not lost in marriage. Rather, marriages should bolster and strengthen the sense of personal worth. Each partner in the marriage is like a pillar holding up the roof of their marriage. If they are placed proportionately away from the center of the structure, the pillars will hold the weight of the roof, each carrying its own share of the load. If the pillars are placed too close together, the roof will tilt and fall.

Male and female contributions to a marriage relationship are like pillars that hold up the marriage relationship. If each carries its own portion of the weight of the relationship, each makes its own contribution to the stability of the marriage.

When a husband is so possessive that his wife loses her identity and clings to his shadow, the relationship becomes warped. Or, when a wife so aspires to an identity outside the relationship, she will fail to fulfill her part of the marriage. In marriage, sharing equally the privileges and responsibilities of the relationship creates harmony.

The wife who is submissive to her own husband as unto the Lord is fulfilling her proper role, defending the territory of the home, and moving in an orbit in which the marriage and family is the central, most important point (Ephesians 5: 22, 33). The husband who loves his wife in the way Christ wants her to be loved brings out the qualities of cooperativeness in the relationship as they together are submissive to the Lord in keeping Him as the object of their affections (vv. 25-31).

Cultural Demands

Each culture places unique requirements on a marriage. In North America, for instance, it is important for a wife to be aware of the cultural expectations on a man. She learns rather quickly that she cannot compete with her husband for a job. They both may be trained for the same profession but they should not both be seeking the top post or same job. Such competition puts a strain on marital relationships that was never intended in the Christian home.

A woman who loves her husband will not question his strength or belittle his courage. Others are attacking him constantly, pointing out his weaknesses and failures. At home he needs reassurance of his adequacies rather than reminders of his deficiencies. This is part of the kindness in love (1 Corinthians 13:4).

One of the psychological differences between the sexes that is most frustrating is the fact that many men do not find it easy to express their emotions or sentiments. They may feel deeply but have not been allowed freedom to express these feelings.

Unfortunately, difficulty in expressing honest emotions develops because of the American saying, "Big boys don't cry." Little boys who don't learn to express honest emotions grow up to be men who do not know how to express love adequately. You don't have to read far in Biblical literature to see that

85

expression of honest emotion is a time-honored privilege, one that the secularization of our time has almost succeeded in wiping out (Genesis 37:34, 35; 43:30-34; 1 Samuel 18:3; 2 Samuel 18:33; John 11:35).

Men need to remember that the wife hopes her husband will show her affection and express his feelings in tangible ways. Actions may speak more loudly than words, but words are necessary for cultivating continuing relationships.

A wife also hopes her husband will share his concerns—hopes, joys, worries, fears—with her. She may not be able to do anything about them, but just to be able to share on a confidential level is reassuring to the wife who is watching her husband's hair take on a salt-and-pepper pattern and lines etch across his aging face. Love does not deepen through the years unless it is expressed. One of the best ways of sharing love is by demonstrating personal concern.

A wife likes to be admired for her competencies. The man who takes notice of the special efforts his wife takes to make things pleasant around the home is one who comes home to variety. Monotony has no place in Christian marriage. Excitement is sustained by the common courtesies of seeing and telling (1 Corinthians 13:5).

A husband is wise to draw on his wife's intelligence and sensitiveness. When he accepts the fact that she thinks differently and that he should discuss his ideas with her, he has a chance to see things in a new perspective. Many times these sharing times become the seedbed of creative ideas that add zest to family living and even cultivate ideas and concepts that can enrich vocational life outside the home. Certainly it is in such sharing that interpersonal relationships are broadened and powers of communication heightened.

Finally, each must respect the other's individuality. Husbands are born, but they are not born to be remade. Frustrated is the wife who thinks she can remake her husband. Husband and wife both must learn to accept each other for *what* and *who* they are, and create the atmosphere necessary for becoming what each is capable of becoming in Christ Jesus. It is in allowing freedom for personal growth that Christian love reaches its highest potential on the human level.

*Henry Brandt and Homer Dowdy, *Building the Christian Home* (Wheaton, Ill.: Scripture Press).

CHAPTER TEN

Values to Live By

Tastes

THE PERSONAL VIEWPOINTS THAT GOVERN our way of life begin in our tastes or preferences, those things we like or dislike. Expressions of tastes or preferences start as opinions and grow into beliefs which are the basis for building an attitudinal system.

An *opinion* is a verbal expression of a weakly held idea or concept. One person says, "It's too cool today." Another says, "I think it is beautiful." Still another declares, "No, it's too warm." Each is speaking from a personal point of preference. Each may be right in light of his past experiences. Such statements of taste or preference reflect personal opinions and suggest the beginnings of an attitude that will tend to make the day pleasant or unpleasant.

Opinions mature into beliefs, those statements that imply acceptance of a proposition or situation. A belief is usually prefixed with the phrase "I believe. . . . " The statement, "I believe it is going to rain," has no bearing on whether it will rain or not; it just reveals the speaker's position on the possibility.

In the Christian home, opinions have a way of developing into beliefs which form the basis for attitudes. Opinions and beliefs of parents are the foundation on which children start building their own attitudes toward life. The atmosphere of the home sets the climate for attitude development and starts young lives out on positive or negative thought patterns. That's why the wise man of old could say, "As he thinketh in his heart, so is he" (Proverbs 23:7).

Attitudes

Attitudes merge thinking and feeling into concepts that motivate to action. As we noted in lesson 5, by definition, an *attitude* is a relatively enduring tendency to respond consistently with feeling to beliefs that have been learned through experience with people, places, objects, ideas, and concepts.

The phrase "relatively enduring tendency to respond" in the definition represents a stance or habitual position which prepares the person to respond. Look at an athlete. Whether he is swimming, golfing, or playing baseball, he has a stance or bodily position in which he stands in order to initiate appropriate action when the signal sounds. So it is with attitudes. Previous experience—or our memory of experience—has a way of getting us positioned to respond to new situations or opportunities of involvement.

Unfortunately, negative thinking becomes a habit. The "I can't," which begins as an opinion, can grow into an attitude by habitual refusal to become involved. The problem lies in the fact that attitudes are relatively enduring and become resistant to change with age and experience. The older we become, the less flexible our attitudes are and the more they restrict our ability to create or innovate.

It is impossible to measure attitudes—they can only be inferred by behavior. It is really unnecessary to ask a person what his attitude is. You can tell by his life-style. In lesson 7, for instance, we considered the woman with the unsaved husband. The word *conversation* in 1 Peter 3:1 means "consistent life-style" or "behavioral attitude." Actually, Peter is saying: " . . . wives, be in subjection to your own husbands; that, if any obey not the word [the Bible], they also may without the word [nagging] be won by the conversation [consistent life-style, demonstration of attitudes] of the wives."

What kind of attitudes should the Christian family be nurturing? Paul has the answer in Philippians 2: 5: "Your attitude should be the kind that was shown us by Jesus Christ" *(Living Bible)*. If we think as Jesus thought, we can live as He wants to live through us in the 20th century. It is to think as Jesus thought that we want to teach our children, so they can develop the kinds of attitudes that are consistent with the Christ life.

Values

As attitudes mature, they develop into the values that form the core of personality. A value system is reflected in the self-structure of the individual, that constellation of attitudes that merge into what a person sees himself being or becoming (Philippians 3:13, 14). Attitudes form a sense of values, and values form one's philosophy of life. As such, value change involves personality change, which is exactly what happens in conversion (2 Corinthians 5:17).

To value Christ is to make Him the goal of affections and to let His will be the chief motivating factor of life. Valuing the values of the kingdom of heaven requires the ordering of priorities around the principles Christ taught (Matthew 13:44-46).

The Sermon on the Mount, for instance, explores the values of the Kingdom by describing how they apply to daily family living. Jesus emphasized how Christians think (Matthew 5:1-12); appear to others (5:13-16); transcend the Law (5:17-24); behave (5:25-48); worship (6:1-18); plan for the future (6:19-34); discipline themselves (7:1-12); and make decisions (7:13-27). If the principles of the Kingdom are valued, they will influence human behavior in thought and deed (attitudes) and demonstrate Christian values in everyday living.

Teaching these values is essential if the home is to be Christian. Moses emphasized that this is an ongoing, daily process in the normal activities of daily living (Deuteronomy 6:7). Paul says the example of word and deed is essential in teaching the values of Christ (Colossians 3:17).

Value Development

It has been observed that "an adult probably has tens of hundreds of thousands of beliefs, thousands of attitudes, but only dozens of values." If opinions grow into beliefs and beliefs into attitudes and attitudes into values, let's see how this development occurs. The goal, of course, is to introduce the values of the kingdom of heaven into the lives of all members of the Christian family.

Value development involves internalization, which is "the process of incorporating something into one's behavior as one's own, not merely conforming or accepting the values of others."[1] Values do not mature by mere conformity; they must be personally adopted as meaningful. Then they are demonstrated away from home as consistently as at home. The process is fivefold:

Receiving. Children must become aware of others and of new activities in which they are not already involved. They must demonstrate a willingness to receive new information about others or activities and listen to ideas about new opportunities. As they become alert to new opportunities in life they have opportunity to explore attitudes that can develop into new valued experiences.

Take going to church, for instance. Children are taken to church long before they have a choice in the matter. It is in being involved in the activities of the church and its members that they begin to form attitudes toward church that can culminate in the ultimate value: Christ. If their early experiences are positive, it is easier for them to internalize the values of the kingdom of heaven. If not, they have difficulties to overcome. To begin with they have no choice, but their church involvement should be satisfying and create a desire for more participation

Responding. Willingness to respond leads to living up to expectations which, generally, leads to satisfaction in the response. In church, this involves attending activities and living by its expectations. This is not because the child *has* to, but because he *wants* to and finds satisfaction in involvement. In their teens, for instance, many young people find their own way to church activities even if their parents are not involved in them. Initiative illustrates responding.

Valuing. At this point the value is accepted as personally important. The participant defines his relationship to the value, shows his preference for it, and makes a commitment to what it stands for. On this level Christ is accepted as the goal value of life and other endeavors are grouped around this core choice. This is where salvation occurs. Deeper commitment at this level may lead to the infilling of the Holy Spirit and accepting a call into Christian service.

Organizing. After commitment has been made to a value, it is necessary to organize the emerging values of life into a consistent pattern. This involves developing a life-style consistent with the claims of Christ and in harmony with the expectations of the family and the body of believers represented in the local church. The task here is to deal with inconsistency and to avoid the "logic-tight" compartments that would lead to engaging in activities contradictory to spiritual values.

Characterization. The peak of value development is the point of characterization when values consolidate into a philosophy of life that is illustrated by a consistent life-style. At this point the person *is* what he professes to believe. He agrees with Paul at this point: "I am crucified with Christ: nevertheless I live; yet not I, but Christ liveth in me: and the life which I now live in the flesh I live by the faith of the Son of God, who loved me, and gave himself for me" (Galatians 2:20).

Teaching Values

Teaching values is one of the most important tasks of parenting (Proverbs 22:6; Ephesians 6:4). For some it is also the most difficult, for many parents fail to see themselves in the role of a teacher. What a parent is and what he does is part of the day-by-day teaching ministry that shares values with a younger generation. Mark 8:36 may correctly be paraphrased: "For what shall it profit a man, if he shall gain the whole world, and lose his own household?"

The following steps in facilitating attitude learning are suggested by Klausmeier and Goodwin and are appropriate for the Christian home:[2]

1. *"Identify the attitudes to be taught."* Recognizing that attitudes can be learned, it is evident that they can be taught. It is the task of the parents to identify the attitudes they want their children to develop and to give opportunity for the attitudes to be cultivated and applied to everyday life.

2. *"Provide exemplary models."* The importance of parents as appropriate models for living and learning should not be underestimated in attitude development. Children's early learning will be through imitation. Parents must take advantage of the early plastic years to mold young lives in the direction of the attitudes of Christ.

3. *"Provide pleasant emotional experiences with attitude objects."* Since positive reinforcement of behavior is more effective than negative reinforcement or punishment, maximum opportunity needs to be provided for children to have pleasant emotional experiences with the people and activities around which attitudes are being cultivated. The Christian life needs to be demonstrated by pleasant individuals engaged in happy, meaningful experiences.

4. *"Extend informative experiences."* The relationship between thinking and feeling is such that the broader the base of meaningful experiences, the more stable the attitudes associated with these experiences. Transferring spiritual concepts to all of

94

life's experiences brings many activities under the influence of attitudes that are being developed. No longer are spiritual attitudes associated just with the church and its people, but the principles of the kingdom of heaven are applied to everyday life and in places far removed from the sanctuary.

5. *"Use group techniques to facilitate commitment."* Attitudes are not developed in a vacuum. The best way to stimulate attitude growth is within the interaction of human relationships. Home, school, church, and community all merge as classrooms for teaching attitudes. At this point it is wise to involve peers and respected elders in the process of attitude development. The social interaction of group learning helps stabilize the attitude base.

6. *"Arrange for appropriate practice."* Practicing attitudes in appropriate situations gives the exercise needed for stimulating attitude growth. This practice must be in a variety of places and usually in connection with group interaction. When attitudes are being learned appropriately, the spiritual principles of the Word will be seen applied in one-to-one relationships, in group settings, and among a variety of groupings in which children are involved.

7. *"Encourage independent attitude cultivation."* Attitude development begins in areas of parental concern but broadens into areas of special concern to the children. It is essential that practice in attitude development branch out to new areas of unique concern to the children. In applying their learning to new situations—not just those set up by their parents —they learn to transfer the spirit as well as the letter of the law to life's activities. As children mature into adulthood the activities of life will change but the

attitudes should remain stable as they are applied to new and unique situations.

How can we know when attitude teaching in the home is being transferred to life outside the home? When we see the young growing up, moving beyond the immediate circle of the family with confidence, and maintaining their faith in Christ as they apply the attitudes of His kingdom to the experiences of everyday life. As this occurs, the 20th-century parent can do as Mary of old did; she "kept all these sayings in her heart" as she watched her Son develop attitudes and actions that were pleasing to the Heavenly Father (Luke 2:51, 52).

---

[1] Herbert J. Klausmeier and William Goodwin, *Learning and Human Abilities*, 2nd ed. (N.Y.: Harper and Row, Publishers, 1966).

[2]*Ibid.*, pp. 120-122.

CHAPTER ELEVEN

Family Togetherness

Leisure and Play

CHILDREN ARE BORN WITH THE CAPACITY for play, but how to play must be learned. Too frequently the pressures of adult living makes people forget how to play effectively. However, the constructive use of leisure time is essential to vital Christian living. God never intended man to work around the clock week in and week out. Even He chose to rest after 6 days of creative activity (Genesis 2:1-3).

Leisure involves play that makes merry and is scriptural (Proverbs 15:13-15, 17; Luke 15:23, 24, 32; James 5:13). Frank Severin has observed that "every small boy knows what it means to play, but so far not a single adult has been able to propose either a definition or an explanation" of play that is generally accepted.*

Enjoying play is not the monopoly of the very young. It remains a challenge for all ages to cultivate constructive leisure activities. "To stop playing is not to grow up," William A. Sadler, Jr. observes, "it is to cease living authentically."

Handling leisure time is essential to constructive family interaction. As we move toward a 4-day work week, handling leisure time will become even more important. It is true that recreation is a change of pace—not necessarily fun and games. Recreation is that which takes us away from the pressures and monotony of everyday living. It needs to be first, restful and, then, constructive. Leisure should be recreative. It should give us new perspectives with which to face old tasks.

From this growth point of view, letting children work alongside their parents can be the kind of play that is instructive. Learning to work can be taught through play if parents have the right attitude toward productiveness. Such activities are essential to mental health and spiritual maturity.

In Deuteronomy 6:7 Moses emphasized that the parents of Israel should teach their children how to love God efficiently and their neighbor effectively when sitting down (table talk), walking about (working and playing together), lying down (evening sharing), and rising up (preparing for a new day).

Creative Leisure

Far too many people are unable to enjoy leisure activities and give themselves wholeheartedly to play without feeling guilty. They feel they should be devoting their time to something more practical, forgetting that when they have taken a break from the pressure of work they can return with new vigor and heightened inspiration.

Families that press a work ethic that makes the young feel guilty for nonwork create the kinds of compulsive personalities that cannot relax when they are older. Such preoccupation with work leads to a circular kind of living that robs life of its rest. Leisure and play are an appropriate part of normal Christian living.

Even though Jesus was active in carrying out the work the Father had sent Him to do, He also spent time in rest (Matthew 8:24, 25); prayer (Matthew 14:23; Mark 6:46; Luke 6:12; 9:28); sharing (Luke 10:38; John 15:14, 15); and enjoying the created universe (Matthew 6:28, 29; Mark 4:3).

Studies indicate that few people experiment with recreations or hobbies in old age that they did not at least experiment with in their childhood or youth. That is why the emphasis in school physical education is shifting from contact sports (football and basketball) to recreations that allow more people to be involved who are less athletic (tennis, archery, ping-pong, golf). The aim is to teach activities that can be enjoyed into middle and older age when physical energies are declining. These must be started in youth, however, if they are to be functional in old age.

Play is intended to be therapeutic. To be therapeutic, play must be grounded in love—love for God the author of life and love for the others with whom we are enjoying the interactions of life. Play, as God intended it to be experienced, is the creative unfolding of one's personal world, a discovering of one's identity.

Play offers us a chance to get a new perspective of who we are in God's universe. Sadler suggests that "creative reorientation through play helps us to be more realistically aware of our world, more objective about ourselves and better prepared to receive new information and insight."

Instead of concentrating on the anxiety that evolves in the work-a-day world, we focus on the creative behaviors that emerge from the love and trust that are a part of creative play activities. This focuses our attention on new possibilities for ourselves and others for living creative lives in the world of work.

Closing the Generation Gap

Playing together is one of the most effective ways of closing the generation gap. To play together, parents and children must live in a common world. It is neither child nor adult—it is a shared world.

Chronological age makes no difference in play where the partners see the opportunity of creating a common history by moving within the same time and space. They exchange insights; they share interpretations of the past, present, and future.

Such play is not a regression to impulsive behavior; it is discovering the richest meanings of sharing together on a human level and developing spiritual appreciation for each other, God, and His universe. Perhaps this is what Christ had in mind when He said, "Except ye . . . become as little children, ye shall not enter into the kingdom of heaven" (Matthew 18:3).

Sound mental health is demonstrated by the ability to give one's self as wholeheartedly to play as to work. For the parent, this involves leaving your work on the job and coming home to shift gears into creative leisure. From this perspective, the home chores can become constructive play when the leisure activities become a basis for involving the children in learning constructive pursuits. For, it is the quality of togetherness that is more important than the quantity of hours spent together.

Parents are advised to involve their children in the work activities of home, yard, and car so they can learn to carry out responsibility and find pleasure in the dignity of work. It may take a little longer to accomplish the task while waiting for little fingers to become coordinated, but it is essential for the welfare of the child and conducive to proper attitude building in the Christian home.

The following are some suggestions for cooperative leisure that is recreative:

1. Adults as well as children should experiment with recreation that they can sustain through their declining years.

2. Children need to be involved in recreational and work activities that are particularly suited to their muscular development. This suggests that household tasks involving arms and legs, such as doing dishes, sweeping, cleaning, and yard duties, should be taught before embroidery or woodworking.

3. Work activities need to be distributed among the children, taking into account their individual differences. Allowances should be made for a preference for indoor or outdoor work so the recreational aspect of productiveness is in focus.

4. Play and recreational activities should be consistent with your spiritual values. This involves various kinds of family play, field trips, outings, sporting events, and cultural activities.

5. Parents need to learn how to enjoy being spectators when their child is a participant, especially in school and church activities and programs.

6. Creative play is one of the ways of teaching discipline; the introduction of control into life (Ephesians 6:1-4). Play should not be viewed as a waste of time, but a special time designed for the recreation of the soul. People who learn to play

adequately make better workers both at home and on the job.

Devotional Togetherness

Having family devotions is one of the most beautiful opportunities for cultivating togetherness as a family. The time and place of family devotions will vary as the children mature. It is essential to keep family living devotional rather than concentrating on the ritual.

With young children, reading stories is appropriate any time during the day, but especially when they are winding down for a nap or bedtime. Bible stories, poems, and choruses offer sterling opportunities to share spiritual truth when they are uniquely receptive. When they are old enough to talk and think, they should be taught to pray and encouraged to formulate their own prayers.

Memorization of songs and Scripture verses comes next as the cognitive abilities of children develop. Such activities should be for the joy of learning. Pressure should not be exerted. Group recitation of Bible passages is a wonderful way to involve the family in devotional sharing. A step removed from this is individual testimonies or prayer requests, phrased in the language of the participant.

When they get into school and are learning to read, Bible reading should be included in devotions. This can start with a modern version of the Bible and then use the King James Version if it is used in church in the ministry of the Word. Begin with a version the child understands—a paraphrase. Include Bible storybooks and branch out to devotional readers and stories of famous Christians of the present and the past.

As the children grow older, they should be included in selecting and reading the Scripture passage as well as praying. A sing-along with the piano or record player adds variety to devotional times and reinforces the musical program of the church.

The time and length of devotions will vary as the children grow older and have more demands outside the home. Whatever time is most convenient for the majority of the family should be considered, whether in the morning, at suppertime, or at bedtime. Involving the children in selecting the devotional time will encourage their cooperation.

It must be remembered, however, that having a regular time of devotions is no substitute for a devotional atmosphere in the home. Parents need to be alert to unique ways and unanticipated times when the claims of Christ can be presented or His attitudes demonstrated.

Together in Spiritual Service

Corporate worship should be seen as an extension of family worship. It is in bringing together the families of the church in worship and evangelism that the church has its true identity. A church will be no stronger than the family units on which it is based, so it is important to work on the stability of the family unit as part of church establishment.

Families that pray together also need to worship together. There is something to be said for the early American custom of the family pew in which mother and father sat together with the children for worship and instruction. This is especially true on communion Sunday. Parents should not only set the example of worship, attitude, and attending to instruction, but should be near at hand to help their young crystallize their beliefs and behaviors concerning spiritual things.

Along with the other fragmentations of the contemporary society has come the breaking of the family unit into small groups meeting in separate rooms or chapels. This may be all right for some of the teaching and expression activities of the church, but there is still something to be said for corporate worship of the whole family assembling together with other families for spiritual growth (Hebrews 10:25).

Togetherness in spiritual service also involves the outreach ministries of the church. This begins in the stewardship of tithing in which each member of the family is taught the meaning of tithing and how to figure his tithe for each pay period. Giving allowances in units of 10 and making payments for special chores in the same manner gives the parents a chance to help their children figure their tithes accurately as a part of their spiritual involvement. Children should have their own tithing envelopes and be encouraged to tithe consistently, following the example of their parents, not only in tithing, but in offerings.

Then there's the stewardship of time. This involves participation in the activities of the church, both graded and nongraded. There is a place for graded activities, especially for instruction by age-groups. When these are balanced by the nongraded times of involvement in which the family interacts together with other families, the spiritual potential of family togetherness is maximized. What has been communicated in the graded sessions can be expressed in the nongraded sessions and all are enhanced.

Capitalizing on the numerous opportunities for

family togetherness gives the Christian family unlimited opportunities for interaction and "instruction in righteousness" (2 Timothy 3:16, 17). What starts at home in play and leisure is brought together in devotions and then implemented in corporate worship. Sharing Christ in these varied activities in which young eyes are watching mature lives maximizes the potential of 1 Corinthians 11:1. Parents can join Paul in saying, "Be ye followers of me, even as I also am of Christ."

---

*Frank Severin, *Discovering Man in Psychology* (N.Y.: McGraw-Hill Book Company, 1973).

CHAPTER TWELVE

Death and Loneliness

Biblical View of Death

TRY NOT TO THINK ABOUT IT as we will, it is appointed to us all to die (Hebrews 9:27). Every family needs to prepare its members to face death and dying. The quality of togetherness a family has will influence how adequately they can adjust to the loss of a family member. The more open and accepting the family interaction, the more easily they can tolerate the separation of illness or death and the subsequent loneliness.

Severin has observed that the person who "is able to perceive significance even in dying should be in a better position to encounter it with calm courage. The earnest Christian who is convinced that "the meaning of life is consummated in its termination' will see death in still a different light."[1] Preparing the family to accept death begins with looking at the Biblical perspective of the event.

The Old Testament teaches that death exists because of sin in the world, but not necessarily because of sin in the life of the one dying (Genesis 2:17). As a result, death is inevitable to all mortals (Genesis 25:11; Joshua 23:14; 2 Samuel 12:23; Job 3:17, 19). In death, the body of man returns to the dust from which he was formed (Genesis 2:7; 3:19; Ecclesiastes 8:10; 12:7).

To the righteous, death is an introduction to a destiny of eternal good, an event to be anticipated by all who know God (Isaiah 45:17; Daniel 7:14; 12:2; Numbers 23:10). Above all, Jehovah God should be viewed as the Creator and Sustainer of life. Confidence in Him gives grace to live by and to die by (Job 19:25-27).

Building on these Old Testament concepts, the New Testament presents death as laying aside the body, and compares it with taking down the tent of a temporary pilgrimage (2 Corinthians 5:1; 2 Timothy 4:6). Again, the New Testament presents the fact that death is in the world because of sin and emphasizes that death comes to everyone (Romans 5:21; 6:23; 1 Corinthians 15:56; Hebrews 2:14; James 1:15).

The suggestion is strong that no correlation can be drawn between the manner of a man's death and God's verdict of the quality of his life—the godly may die violently and the ungodly may die quietly of natural causes (Matthew 5:45). For the Christian, the death trauma is to be viewed as a glorious experience leading to union with Christ (2 Corinthians 5:4; 1 Thessalonians 4:13-15). Unbelievers, on the other hand, can only anticipate eternal torment (Matthew 25:46; Mark 3:29; 2 Thessalonians 1:9; Jude 7; Acts 1:25).

Overshadowing the New Testament view of death is the fact that Christ conquered death in His atoning sacrifice and removed the sting from death (John 5:24; 1 Corinthians 15:53-57; 1 John 5:20; Revelation 1:18; Romans 7:24, 25; Revelation 14:13; Hebrews 9:27; Revelation 20:4-6, 11-13). Anticipating the future, the righteous dead are pictured as awaiting resurrection (Luke 16:22, 23; 2 Corinthians 5:8; Philippians 1:21-24).

Contemporary Perspectives

In too many families today a death-denying attitude prevails. People avoid the subject of death with the false assumption that it will occur "to thee and to thee but not to me." This denial of death is part of the idolatry of materialism that exists in our culture. Such a view of death is inconsistent with the awareness that Christ is Lord and that He is the center of the Spirit-motivated life.

Kastenbaum observes that the trend is to "isolate and punish the dying. We try to reclaim our conscience by purchasing elaborate funerals, or we try to blink death out of our minds with skimpy memorial services. We forget the dead—and then are haunted by them."[2]

Dr. Kubler-Ross, who has worked with hundreds of terminal patients, suggests that "in our unconscious, death is never possible in regard to ourselves. It is inconceivable for our unconscious to imagine an actual ending of our own life here on earth, and if this life of ours has to end, the ending is always attributed to a malicous intervention from outside by someone else. In simple terms, in our conscious mind we can only be killed; it is inconceivable to die of a natural cause or of old age. Therefore death in itself is associated with a bad act, a frightening happening, something that in itself calls for retribution and punishment."[3]

A more appropriate view of death for the contemporary Christian is to see the normalcy of the experience. Death is a *natural event*. President John Quincy Adams perceived death from this point of view. When he was 80 he was asked how he was. He replied: "John Quincy Adams is quite well. But the house where he lives is becoming dilapidated. It is tottering. Time and seasons have nearly destroyed it, and it is becoming quite uninhabitable. I shall move out soon. But John Quincy Adams is quite well, thank you."

Death is also a *personal event*—it is not something that merely happens to you. You are a participant in the experience. Although it may be novel to the one undergoing the experience, it is not new to mankind. Contrary to common belief, death is not painful. Actually, it is total freedom from pain.

Death is a *social event*. It seldom occurs in isolation. Death occurs within a community of friends and relatives, usually with some of them present. As such, death serves as a point of bringing families together. For the Christian, this is a wonderful time for letting the spiritual light shine. Whether we want to admit it or not, our behavior at the time of death and our actions at the Christian funeral serve to reinforce our testimony to the unbelieving world.

Further, death is a *mystery*. Even when we try to imagine what death would be like, man is still aware that he is the thinking subject. Actually, it is impossible for us to contemplate life after death, so we see it as an extension of the here and now. It is into this mystery that the Lord steps, taking the believer to be forever with Him (1 Corinthians 15:51-57; 1 Thessalonians 4:13-17). Death should be viewed as the fulfillment of life (2 Corinthians 5:8).

Preparing the Family

Parents should not wait until a loved one dies to introduce the concept of death to children. Teaching the acceptance of death must be developmental if it is to avoid the trauma of suddenness. Children need to be prepared for the loss of aging relatives (especially grandparents) and friends. Lead them into the awareness that this life is not eternal and that all must face the transition of death sooner or later. If children can be introduced to the concept of death through natural causes and physical deterioration, it will be easier to help them accept premature death by accident.

Children need to be introduced to funeral customs and the religious rituals surrounding death. Parents are advised not to wait until the death of a family member to take a child to his first funeral or introduce him to the mortuary and its functions. When such introductions are made through the death of acquaintances, it will be easier to involve them in the funeral services of close relatives. Here is where parents can set the example of their faith and let their funeral behavior demonstrate the faith of the believer in the loving eternality of Christ.

By introducing the normal sequence of death in terminal illness, it will be easier to handle accidental and premature death. Children have to realize that the anticipated 70 years of life is not extended to everyone. There are premature deaths. Some are from disease, some from accident, some apparently from causes unknown. Children who perceive God as a loving Father can accept the fact that He chose to take a relative early and not blame God as a villain in robbing them of a valued friendship.

Parents should take precautions to have a valid will to cover the family in case of a premature death. Legal services should be secured to make sure the will makes adequate provision for the economic matters of the family (surviving adults as well as minor children). Guardians should be selected for the children to ensure that they will have the right kind of spiritual guidance in the event both parents are killed. The will should also include the work of the Lord as a continuing participation in stewardship.

It is also wise for families to discuss funeral plans before they are needed. This should involve the type of funeral, cost of services, place of service and burial, participants in the memorial service, and the musical selections to be used. If these arrangements are not made leisurely, many decisions will have to be made on the spur of the moment. All that can be done to ease the situation for the survivors is a demonstration of love on the part of the departed one.

Such discussions are not morbid. Rather, they are a demonstration of our awareness that we all must meet our Maker sometime. It is a demonstration to young lives of what it means to be ready at all times (Romans 6:23).

Handling Loneliness

Loneliness is a condition of the human existence. It is necessary for everyone to recognize loneliness; to be aware of what it means to be utterly alone. To fight such an awareness is to attempt to escape an essential quality of the human existence. It is in facing loneliness that we can grow to our ultimate potential as Jesus did when He faced the reality of the impending cross where He felt deserted by the Father (Mark 15:34).

The loneliness that sweeps over the survivor following the death of a loved one can be devastating or invigorating, depending on how one perceives the emotion. To fight loneliness is to drop into deep despair, a gnawing, captivating feeling of aloneness for which there is no cure. David had to fight this feeling and by so doing discovered the hope that comes to the survivor who has faith in God (2 Samuel 12:15-23).

The secret to handling loneliness is to learn to be alone without being lonely. An awareness of divine friendship is a comfort in the alone hours when God is perceived as present and closer than family (Joshua 1:5; Proverbs 18:24; Hebrews 13:5, 6). A study of creativity indicates that most inventions that demonstrate true originality were constructed while the designer was alone and had free command over his creative powers.

Loneliness that is not channeled creatively is devastating to the personality. It is more intense than hunger, thirst, or insomnia. It leads to emotional deterioration that borders on despair and results in emotional paralysis and helplessness. It is this kind of loneliness that must be shunned by the believer. This can only be done by prayer, Bible study, and active involvement with others in spiritual activities. Rather than succumb to the loneliness that accompanies death, the survivor needs to take stock of the situation and let the Holy Spirit teach him to handle aloneness creatively so as not to be gripped by loneliness (Philippians 4:13; 1 John 4:4).

Being alone without being lonely is a challenge to faith and one of the most vital testimonies to the unbelieving world of the reality there is in Christ and the validity of His claims upon human existence.

Pure Religion

It is in ministering to the lonely that Christianity reaches its purest display in the community (James 1:27). Children should be involved in visitation of the bereaved. They need to realize that the whole family of believers—no matter what their age—has a ministry to the survivors. Such activities as visitation, sharing food, and participating in household activities are a practical demonstration of what it means to be part of the brotherhood of believers.

Too frequently the church is attentive at the time of death but fails to remember in the days following the funeral that time drags heavily for the bereaved. When visits to the home are made regularly and the bereaved are invited outside the home for active participation in the community, the lonely are given new things to think about. Hopes and ambitions can be rekindled to pick up the pieces of life and chart a positive future.

Children who are involved in such practical demonstrations of religious fellowship are given a new glimpse of what it means to be part of the family of God. Such involvement will have a stabilizing effect on their lives. The result: everyone is helped because pure religion is being demonstrated and divine strength flows through the spiritual community.

A side effect of helping all members of the family be aware of the tenuousness of life is to make each member of the family search his own heart to be sure of his spiritual condition. Morbid preoccupation with death is not the point. It is merely being aware of the fact that each member of the family will die sooner or later (Hebrews 9:27). The daily task is to be prepared so whether the time comes early in life or much later, each member of the household is ready to meet Christ.

We cannot really live until we have settled the death question. Then it is possible to realize that faith in Jesus Christ is more than a faith to die by—it is a faith to live by. When this concept dawns in each mind, the constant joy of living by faith in the faith makes each day filled with the presence of the Lord. Such an attitude prepares each member of the family for His coming, be it through death or the Rapture (Luke 12:40).

---

[1] Frank Severin, *op. cit.*

[2] Robert Kastenbaum and Ruth Aisenberg, *The Psychology of Death* (N.Y.: Springer Publishing Company, Inc., 1972).

[3] Elizabeth Kubler-Ross, *On Death and Dying* (N.Y.: Macmillan Company, 1969).

CHAPTER THIRTEEN
Untying the Apron String

UNTYING THE APRON STRING begins in the attitudes of young lovers before the first child arrives. They must totally accept each other, without the conditions, possessiveness, deceitfulness, and insecurity of fragmenting love (lesson 7).

It is in the mutual accepting of each other's differences, which represent both assets and liabilities in their relationship, that they can be open with each other and with God. When He is the Head of the household and the young couple sees each other as gifts to each other from Him, the stage is set for welcoming children who will grow up in the atmosphere of accepting love (Philippians 4:5-7).

The first years of marriage have been called the "establishment phase." This is the period extending from the wedding until the first pregnancy. It is the time in which the two become one psychologically as well as physically. Their areas of compatibility enlarge to make a comfortable, accepting home into which new life can be welcomed.

This is the period in which the young couple establishes their home and develops a pattern of living together as a couple, a family of two. As they integrate their goals and ambitions and share their joys and sorrows, they develop an atmosphere of acceptance which reaches out beyond their immediate concerns to meaningful relationships with members of the extended family and the community. Such diverse interaction prepares them psychologically for the demands of parenthood.

The "expectant phase" of family living extends from the first awareness of pregnancy until the birth of the first child. During this time the family must reorganize its patterns of interaction and restructure the budget. Both expectant parents undergo an "enlargement of the heart" which permits their love to expand to such dimensions that it can accept a new life without robbing each other of the security that comes in loving relationships.

Preparing for the arrival of the first child is an exciting time. It is also psychologically stressful because of the new emotions experienced along with the physical changes that come with pregnancy.

With all of the physical and emotional preparations for the anticipated arrival, there must be a spiritual preparation of the couple. Both must be careful to keep their personal devotional lives vital and their family devotions meaningful. Spiritual preparation for parenthood is essential if the family is to be Christ-centered. The arrival of the newborn should add to the spiritual dimension of the relationship because the new life is a testimony to the creative power of God which has shared new life with the expectant couple (Exodus 2:1-10).

Dependence

Next are the child-rearing years in which the infant is the center of attention. This period lasts about 30 months, taking the child through the era of rapid physical growth leading to crawling, walking, talking, and elimination control. It is a period in which the child is totally dependent on the parents to meet his needs.

Studies indicate that the first 3 years are the most crucial in the emotional life of a child. The beginning of adult patterns of life are crystallized in this early period of dependence. Quality parenting at this time is essential if the child is to grow to be a healthy, normal person. There is no substitute for adequate parenting from both mother and father in this period. Children should not be left to the primary care of strangers during this crucial time. And, parents must see themselves as teachers so as to introduce the right basic system of control into the life of the child.

The developmental task of the first year of life is developing trust—trust of parents and a friendly world. Otherwise, the child becomes mistrusting. This leads to insecurity which later demonstrates itself as inferiority. During years 2 and 3 the task is developing autonomy. Otherwise, shame and guilt will stalemate learning (Proverbs 22:6).

Husband-wife relations must be reevaluated during this time, establishing a new system of communication that does not neglect each other while tending to the ever growing demands made by the growing child. Relationships with the extended family and community must also be revised and the restrictions that come with having a baby around the house must be accepted without a feeling of deprivation.

The next phase lasts from about 30 months to 5 years of age or entering kindergarten. This is the preschool period in which the child is more mobile and verbal. The task here is developing initiative rather than guilt which impedes emotional growth.

At no point in this dependence era should the couple lose sight of the fact that they are lovers. God does not send children into the home to fragment it. The couple needs to continue having time for each other and a variety of activities together outside the home. Using a sitter for nights out and the nursery for church services is good. Making excursions as a threesome is also essential to keeping togetherness alive during the half-decade of preschool family living.

Love stays alive only as long as it is expressed. The Lord does not expect a couple to ignore their relationship in order to meet the needs of a child. Rather, the child should be a means of bringing the couple together in a variety of experiences that make their marriage more wholesome. The right approach to parenthood sees young life as an extension of life that draws parents together in a new dimension (Psalms 127; 128).

Independence

Independence starts in the preschool period the first time the child says, "Let me do it," when an adult tries to do something for him. It is normal and should be allowed to grow into creative initiative. Independence intensifies in the elementary school years and reaches its climax during adolescence. These 6 or 7 years are filled with opportunities in which the child needs to develop a sense of industry, using his own creativity and ingenuity in experimenting with life. If he is not given the freedom of such exploration, a sense of inferiority develops which stunts growth mentally and emotionally.

Giving a child the psychological latitude to develop his own initiative, gifts, and talents places a strain on the family. However, such freedom is essential if the child is to feel he is capable of handling the privileges and responsibilities of life. Taking the initiative in learning is conducive to creative living.

This is the period in which children need to see faith in action. The lives of their parents either reinforce spiritual truths or raise questions of inconsistency (1 Peter 3:15; Ephesians 5:15). Family devotions and active participation in spiritual experiences are essential for adequate spiritual maturity (Psalm 119:164). Many children at this age make their first steps toward identification with Christ and His kingdom. This should be voluntary, however, because the child's concept of God is still immature.

As the child matures with nurturing experiences, he can come to see God as a loving Father who sent Christ to die for the sins of mankind. Children should be exposed to spiritual truth, but not forced to a confrontation of commitment until they have developed the cognitive skills to handle the claims of such a declaration (1 Corinthians 13:11).

Parents must work hard during their children's elementary school years to maintain a vital marital relationship. Otherwise, when the tide of adolescence hits the home, they will not be prepared for it. During adolescence the child must not only know that he is loved and accepted at home—he must reach out into the peer world and find acceptance among his age-mates.

Parents must develop their relationship with each other to stand together against the pressures of the world which would distract youth from the values of a Christian heritage. Parents who have maintained an active love for each other and a vital faith in Jesus Christ can handle the stress of adolescence in their children and find they are growing together, not being drawn apart.

The developmental task of the adolescent is finding his own identity as a person, male or female, and making the adjustment society requires of the sexes. It is also a time of learning to experience the physical and chemical changes occurring in the body and interpreting them as God's approval indicating that the boy is becoming a man, the girl a woman, with all the privileges and responsibilities that maturity entails (Hebrews 2:18).

Interdependence

The choices of adolescence, which lead to career and marriage, bring youth to a place of recognizing they have attained the privileged place of making independent decisions. It also brings the realization that they they still have roots buried deep in the nurturing family. This is when interdependence dawns and the youth, rather than rupturing the relationship, unties the apron string with the help of understanding parents. He can then establish a home that is separate but not alienated from the childhood home (Ephesians 6:1-3; Colossians 3:20).

The task for the maturing youth is to develop the capacity to interact intimately with others and to establish an affectionate relationship that will lead to marriage and family. If freedom is not given for such normal maturing the person may isolate himself from society and become a frustrated, unfulfilled individual.

The task of the parents during this period is to mature in their relationship with each other so they can adjust to their children leaving home and still have a vital marriage. The temptation is to become so absorbed with the children during the developmental years that the parents become almost strangers during the child-rearing years.

The plan of God for the Christian family is for the couple to retain a close relationship through all the growing years; giving the children what they need but not robbing from the marriage. When the young are gone, the parents must have a vital relationship with each other.

Parents should work regularly during these years to keep communication open and a system of activities outside the home so they will have a solid base of interaction to continue when they are alone as a couple again. After all, for most couples the years alone after the last child is gone usually number more years than were involved in child rearing.

In the years of middle age when the children are gone and establishing their own homes, the couple that has kept Christ as the center of their relationship and has remained friends as well as lovers will be able to enjoy the fruits of their labors. Adapting to the "empty nest" is easier when the couple see themselves as best friends and vital individuals who are still growing in their potential as unto the Lord. By this time they will realize they have untied the apron string and·yet retain a love for their children.

This is the period of expanding interests and concerns not only for the benefit of the parents, but also for the generation that is following directly in their footsteps. Work productiveness must be fulfilling or stagnation sets in. During these middle productive years the generativity of meaningful work brings a satisfaction for the time and energy that has been expended. It also sets an example for the younger generation to follow as they enter their own vocational careers (Ecclesiastes 9:10; Ephesians 6:5-9; Colossians 3:22).

Finally, the family realizes that it is aging and the retirement years are closing in. The person who has loved selflessly, worked constructively, and lived creatively can look at the opportunity of slowing down the pace of living and enjoy the sense of integrity that comes through the triumphs and disappointments of maturing through life. It is a time of *being* more than doing, of sharing rather than earning. If life has not been rewarding, despair can set in, but that is not necessary in the Christian personality.

The individual who accepted Christ early and has lived by the principles of the kingdom of heaven will find that life has been good to him. He will have become, through joys and sorrows, a trusting, autonomous person whose initiative and industry have brought him to a place of knowing who he is and where he is going. He will have developed the capacity of intimate relationships with selected others and be enjoying the fruits of generative work.

Now he can bask in the glow of having lived a rich, full life and find joy in watching the third generation come along. All of a sudden he has new incentives to extend a helping hand to a new generation of life that is reaching up for guidance into the dimensions of a strange new world.

Reflection

Looking back over a life well lived brings many

emotions. There will have been successes. There will have been failures. There will have been joys. There will have been sorrows (2 Timothy 4:6-8). But, the husband and wife who have maintained the quality of their relationship will find that they have been drawn closer together rather than driven apart.

It comes to some as a shock, but the divorce rate increases about the 25th year of marriage. Students of human behavior have concluded that many couples have turned their attention from each other to their children during the child-rearing years. Then, when the last child is gone, the parents look at each other as strangers because they have not cultivated their own relationship during the busy years of family obligations.

To keep the marriage intact as God intended, couples are advised to work on the quality of their relationship every day, week, month, and year of their marriage. Only then can they enjoy the integrity that is earned when the divine order of priorities is maintained throughout life.

This is why Paul said a man should love his wife and teach his children, why a wife is told to reverence her husband and love her children, and why children are told to honor and obey their parents (Ephesians 5:22 to 6:4; Colossians 3:17-21). These relationships, maintained with a spontaneous love for God, guarantee that life can be lived fully at each stage.

There is no need to stop growing. There is no need to regress to the behavior of an earlier stage. Keep growing as a person. Keep growing as a couple. Keep growing as a family. Keep growing as a Christian. If you do, seeking God's kingdom first, all the joys that are your right as a child of God and joint-heir with

Jesus Christ will be yours as a person, as a parent, and as a Christian (Matthew 6:33; Romans 8:14-17). You will find that children can grow into the independence of adulthood without rupturing family relations. And the apron string will hang loosely with the closeness of continuing relationships.

Aging parents can then turn to their children to provide for them, and find that the tables may have been turned, but the loving parent-child relations of adolescence can make beautiful child-parent relations in later years. Looking back over this life fully lived it will still be true: "It is more blessed to give than to receive" (Acts 20:35).